PIANO PRONTO®

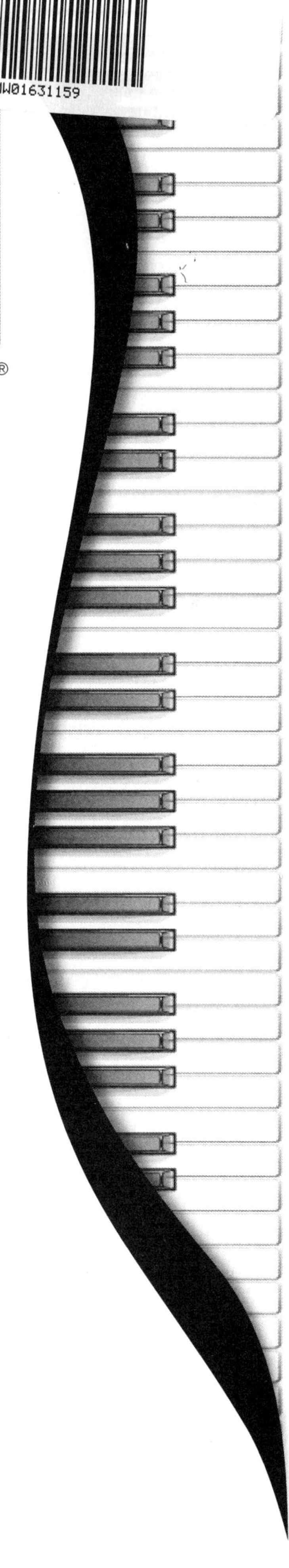

Movement 1

Power Pages™

Materials by

Jennifer Eklund

PIANO PRONTO PUBLISHING

PianoPronto.com

Movement 1: Power Pages

Jennifer Eklund

ISBN 978-1-942751-78-6

Printed in the United States of America.

Piano Pronto Publishing, Inc.
PianoPronto.com

Movement 1

Power Pages

TABLE OF CONTENTS

Foreword

Welcome to *Movement 1: Power Pages*! This book is intended as an all-in-one supplement for the *Movement 1* method book. It follows the same trajectory and presents written theory drills, sightreading, composition, ear training, lead-sheet playing, and other exercises.

When do I use this book? The Power Pages are numbered to correlate with the pieces in the *Movement 1* method book. The Power Pages should be used *after* introducing the corresponding piece in the method book. The exercises augment the materials presented in the method book and in some cases give students a "head start" on new concepts that will be introduced in the next lesson.

What is the format? This book follows a general format that varies slightly between lessons:

***Ready to Review*:** Most lessons begin with a review section that includes short written theory exercises to reinforce theory concepts that have already been introduced. This section is sometimes followed by the introduction of a related concept that expands upon the theory students are encountering in their music.

***Lead the Way!*:** These exercises introduce lead-sheet playing. In the early lessons, students learn to play simple melodies and improvise the left-hand chords by reading chord symbols and using chord options that are provided. As they progress through the book, the chord options gradually disappear, and students are asked to write out their own lead sheets by first harmonizing a melody and then adding appropriate chord symbols.

***Power Play*:** These excerpts always relate to the correlating piece in the method book and exercise the students' reading skills and ability to properly implement fingerings. This section can also double as technique work and allow the teacher flexibility to delve into technical mechanics as needed and depending on the student's readiness.

***Composition Corner*:** These templated composition prompts are designed to kick-start creativity and train handwriting skills.

***I'm All Ears!*:** Short ear-training exercises strengthen the theory concepts introduced in both the method book and the correlating Power Pages. These sections also drill proper handwriting skills.

***Ahead of Schedule*:** These sections preview of a concept students will learn in their next method book piece and allow them to prepare this new skill.

***Analyze This*:** These sections provide a gentle gateway into the world of music analysis via investigating short musical excerpts. They prepare students for the more detailed analysis that they will encounter in future theory workbooks.

Supplemental lessons: A great deal of music theory is introduced in this volume. Supplemental lessons detailing triads, inversions, and musical analysis follow Lessons 19, 20, and 22. Breaking these explanations and exercsises into separate worksheets was necessary in order to thoroughly explain and give students ample review. The concepts introduced in this book apply directly to the music students are playing in the *Movement 1* method book. While it may feel like a lot of theory is presented at once, these ideas will be reviewed thoroughly in the forthcoming Power Pages for *Movement 2* and *Movement 3*.

The C and G major scales are introduced in contrary motion because the fingering is mirrored. For students who are ready to tackle scales in parallel motion, these are provided at the end of the book for all of the tonal centers introduced: C major, G major, and F major.

Just the Basics*

♫ ***Write the letters of the music alphabet in the spaces provided.***

A ____ ____ ____ ____ ____ ____

♫ ***Write the correct beat value under each rhythm or rest below.*****

***Assume a 4/4 time signature.*

♫ ***Match each symbol with the correct name and definition.***

mf	**mezzo piano**	**loud**
p	**forte**	**medium soft**
mp	**piano**	**medium loud**
f	**mezzo forte**	**soft**

**Use before page 4 of the student book.*

Just the Basics*

♫ ***Draw the missing barlines according to the time signatures.***

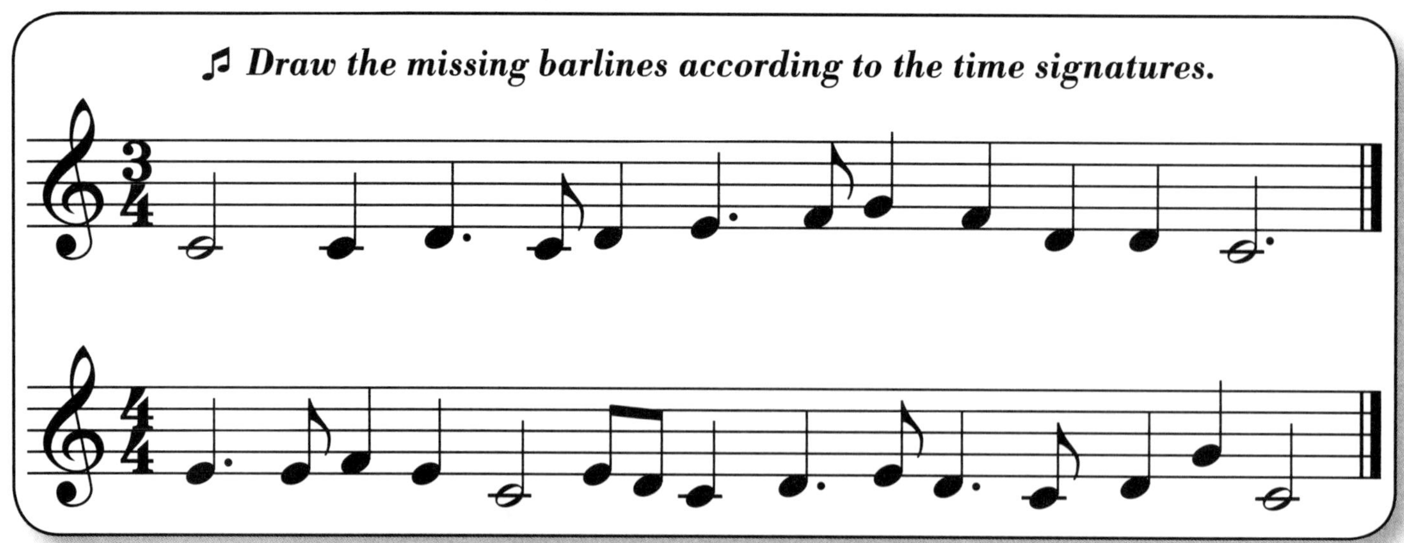

Stem Rules

Single notes BELOW the third line go up on the right side. Notes ON or ABOVE the third line go down on the left side. When two notes are stacked, stem direction is determined by the note that is farthest from the third line.

1. If the notes form a second, the stem is placed in the middle of the notes.
2. For all other harmonic intervals, the stem goes on the side of the notes.

♫ ***Add stems to the treble clef notes below using the stem rules.***

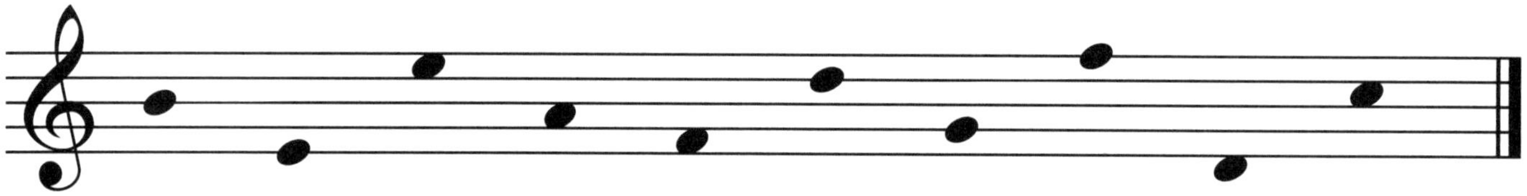

♫ ***Add stems to the bass clef seconds using Rule 1 above.***

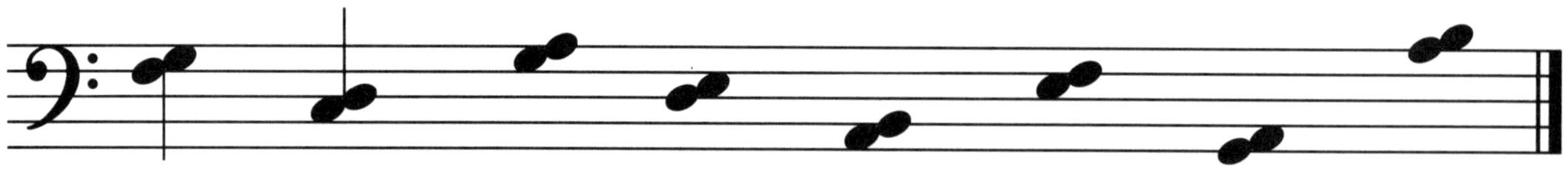

♫ ***Add stems to the treble clef combinations below using Rule 2 above.***

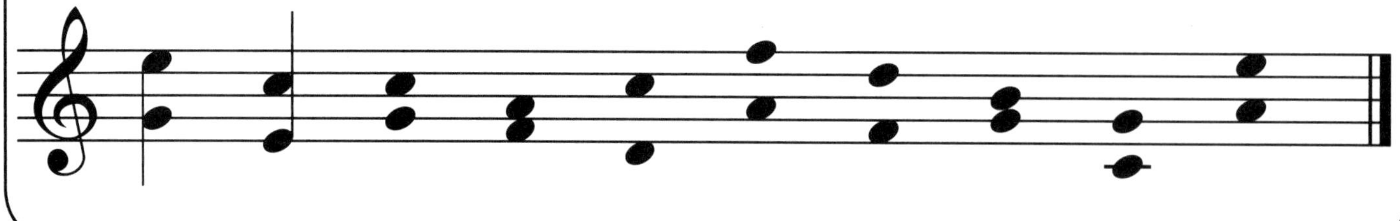

**Use before page 4 of the student book.*

Introduction to Lead Sheets*

A **lead sheet** is a type of sheet music notation that includes a melody on a single staff, and **chord symbols** above the staff that signal which left-hand notes should be played.

Why are you learning to play from a lead sheet?

1. If you were to ever play the piano in a contemporary group setting, like a worship band or a jazz band, you would most likely be expected to play from a lead sheet instead of a traditionally notated piece of music with the treble and bass clef parts written out.

2. Lead sheets are great for gaining a more thorough understanding of music theory, especially chords and chord progressions.

3. Lead sheets are fun! Because the left-hand part is not written out, this gives you the creative freedom to do what you like. As you learn about new ways to play chords, you will find that you have endless possibilities and will never play a piece the same way twice.

In the early lessons of this book, the chord options for the *Lead the Way!* exercises will always be provided for you, notated in the bass clef. Study the example below to learn a few general rules about playing from a lead sheet.

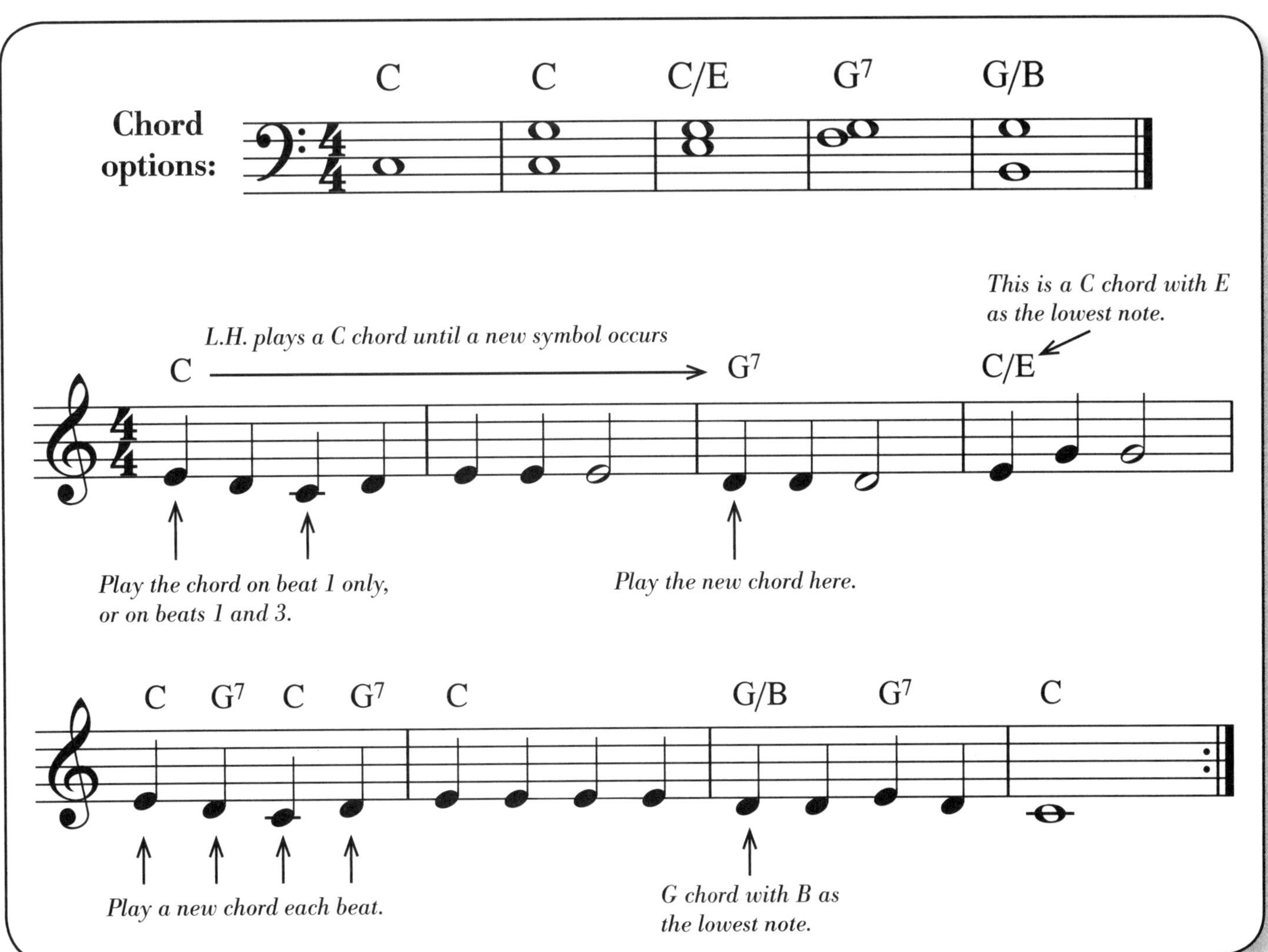

*Use with page 4 of the student book.

1a. Ready to Review

♫ ***Add a C with the correct number of beats to the final measures.***

1b. Lead the Way!

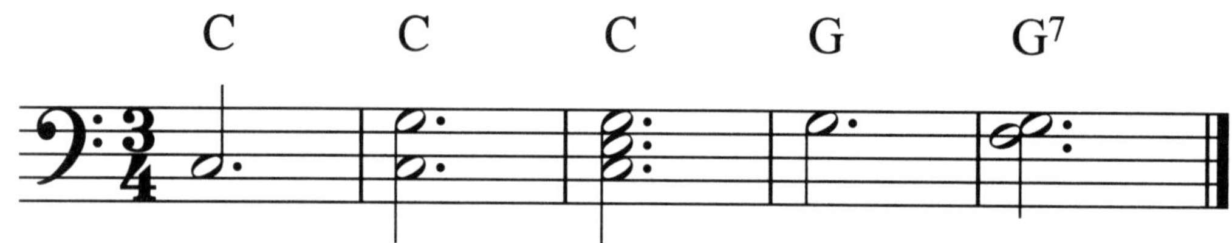

♫ ***Play the melody and improvise the left hand using the given chord symbols and the options above.***

**Reminder: the C chord is sustained through measure 2 even though it is not re-marked. You can choose to hold the chord option you played in measure 1, re-strike it, or play a new one on the first beat of measure 2.*

1c. Power Play

♫ ***Play the examples below. Use the fingerings provided.***

EXAMPLE 1:

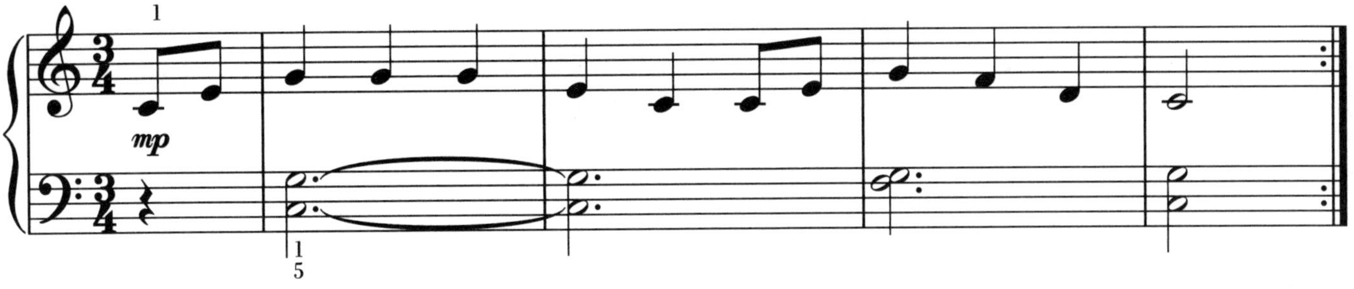

EXAMPLE 2:

1d. Composition Corner

♫ ***Complete the empty measures to compose a short melody. Add chord symbols, using the options on page 5, and play again, improvising with the left hand.***

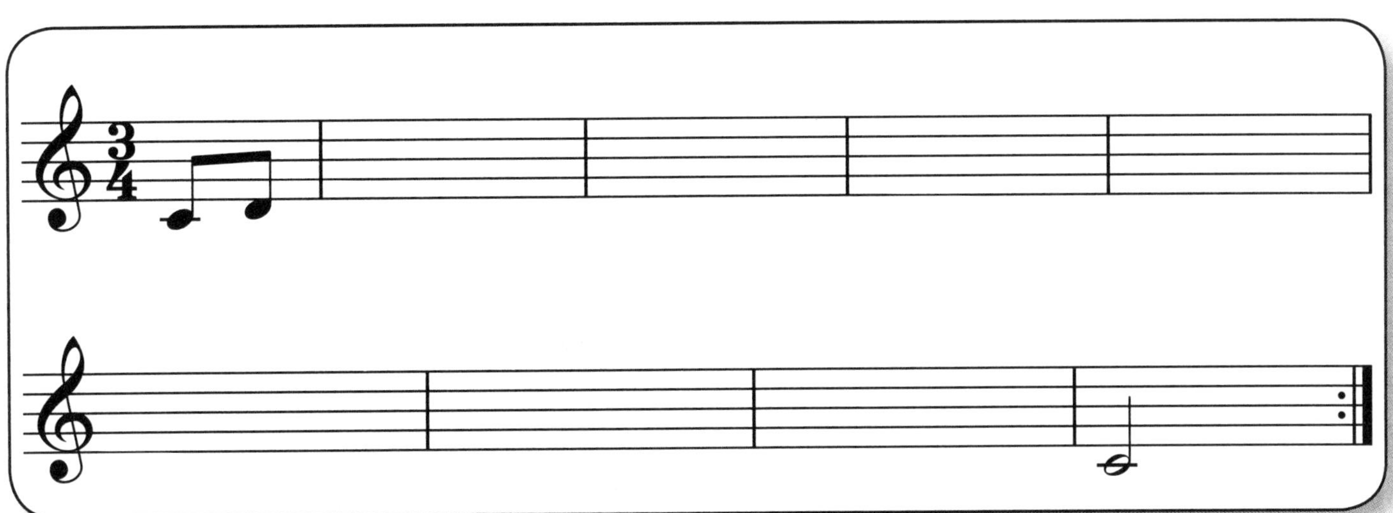

2a. Ready to Review

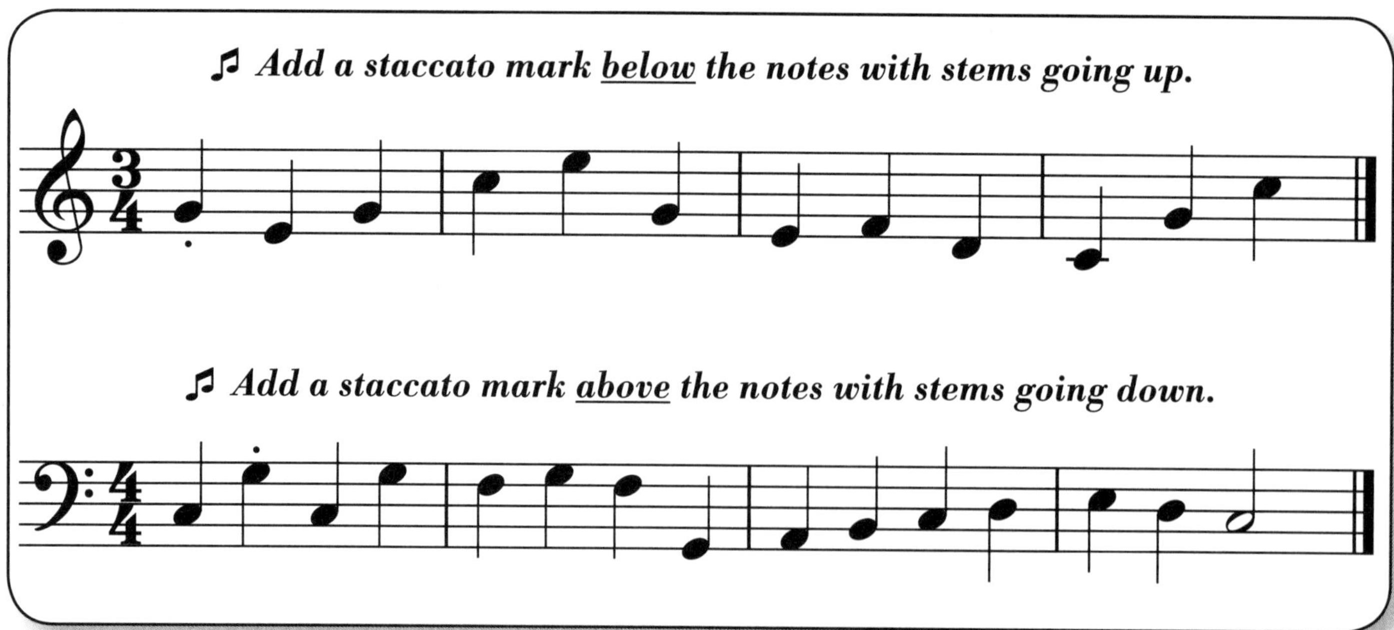

2b. Lead the Way!

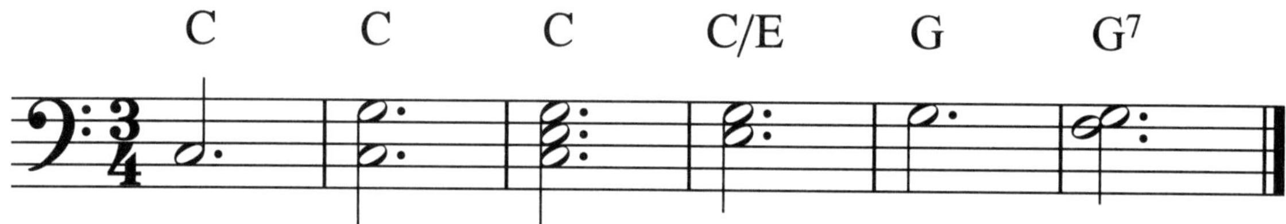

Follow the directions to complete the piece below.

1. Add stems to all of the notes and trace the slurs.
2. Play the melody, and then add chord symbols.
3. Play again and improvise the left hand using the chord symbols.

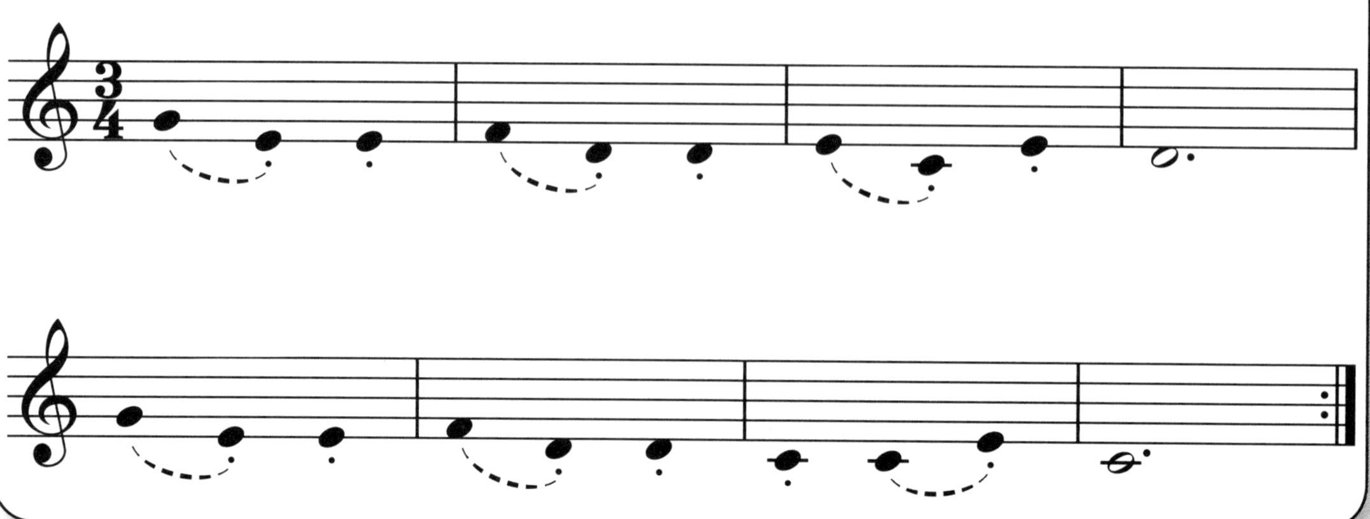

2c. Power Play

♫ *Play the examples below. In the third example, improvise the left-hand chords.*

EXAMPLE 1:

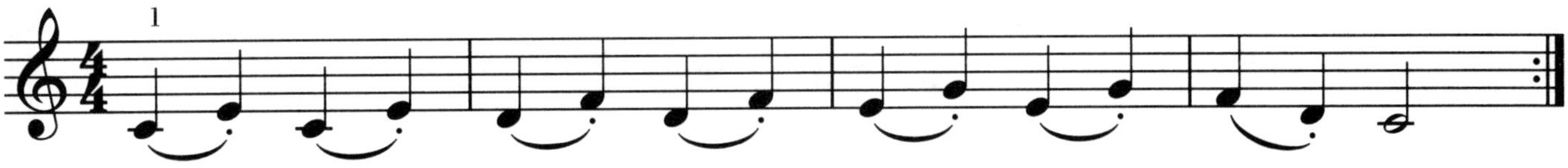

EXAMPLE 2:

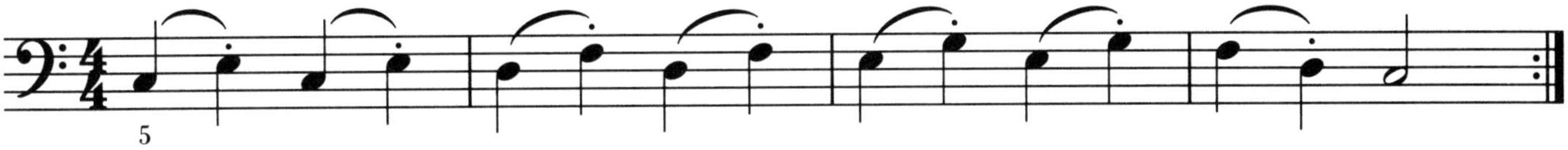

EXAMPLE 3:

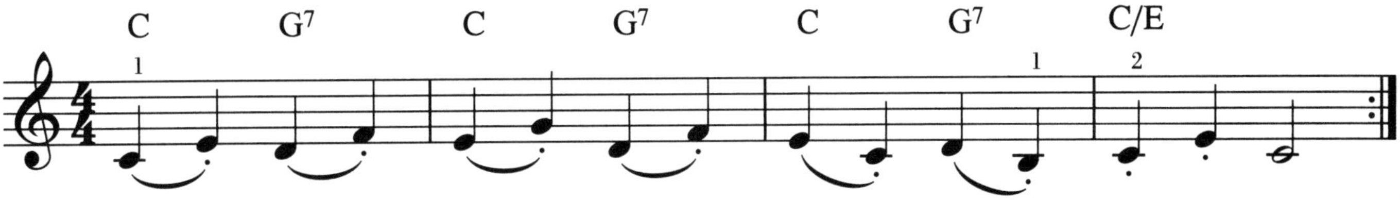

C G7 C G7 C G7 C/E

2d. I'm All Ears!

♫ *Your teacher will play one example from each line. Circle what you hear.*

3a. Ready to Review

♫ ***Label the type of motion in each measure as parallel, contrary, or neither.***

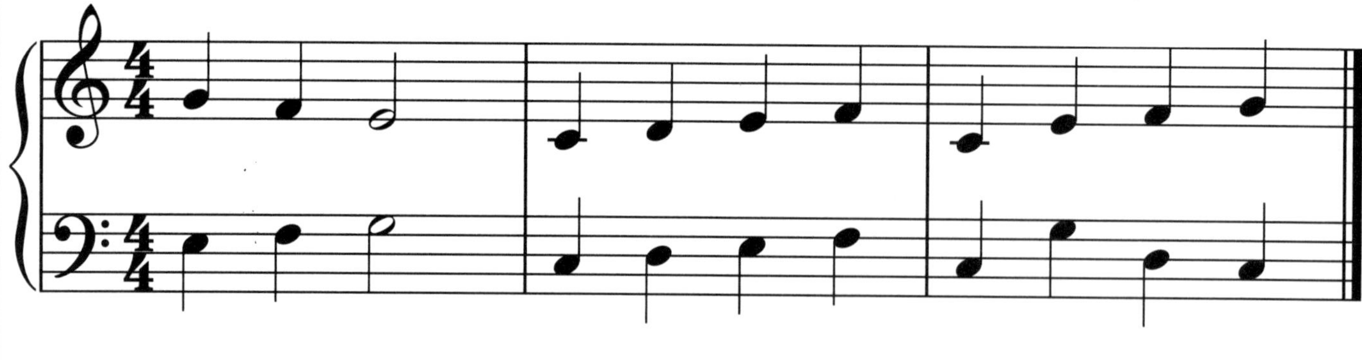

♫ ***Complete the labeled measures by adding bass-clef notes in parallel or contrary motion.* Play the piece.***

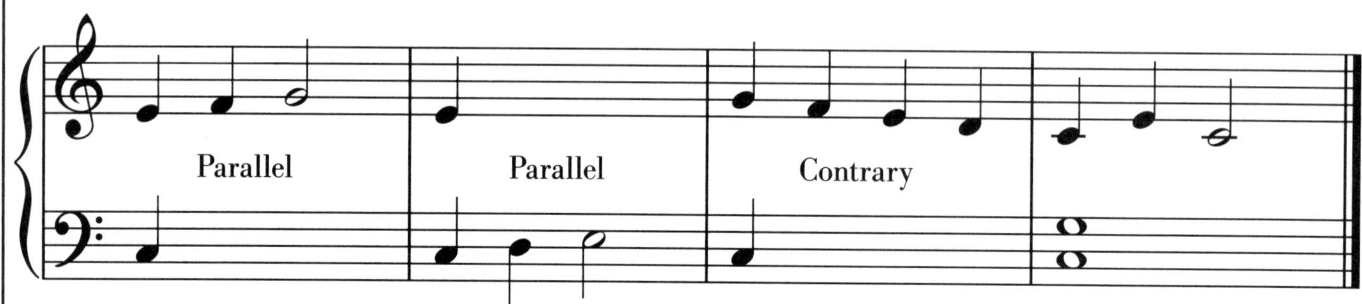

**Use strict contrary motion: notes moving in opposite directions by the same intervals.*

3b. Power Play

♫ ***Play the examples below. Use the fingerings provided.***

EXAMPLE 1:

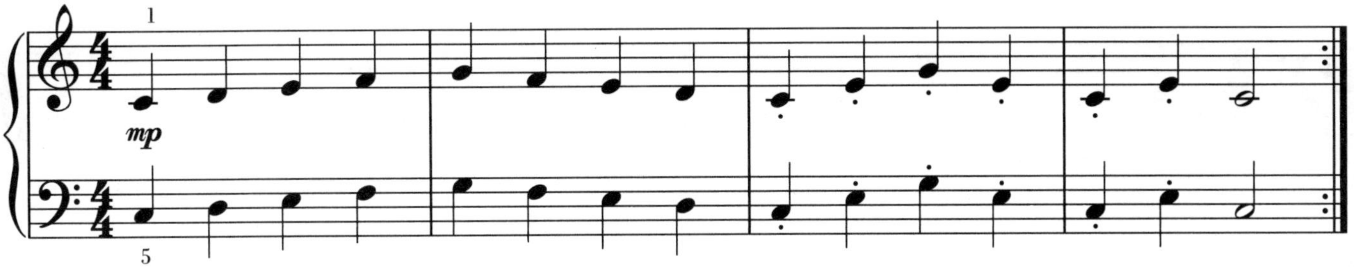

1

mp

5

EXAMPLE 2:

1

mf

1

3c. Composition Corner

♫ ***Complete the piece below by adding left-hand notes in parallel or contrary motion as indicated. Add staccatos and slurs, and then play the piece.***

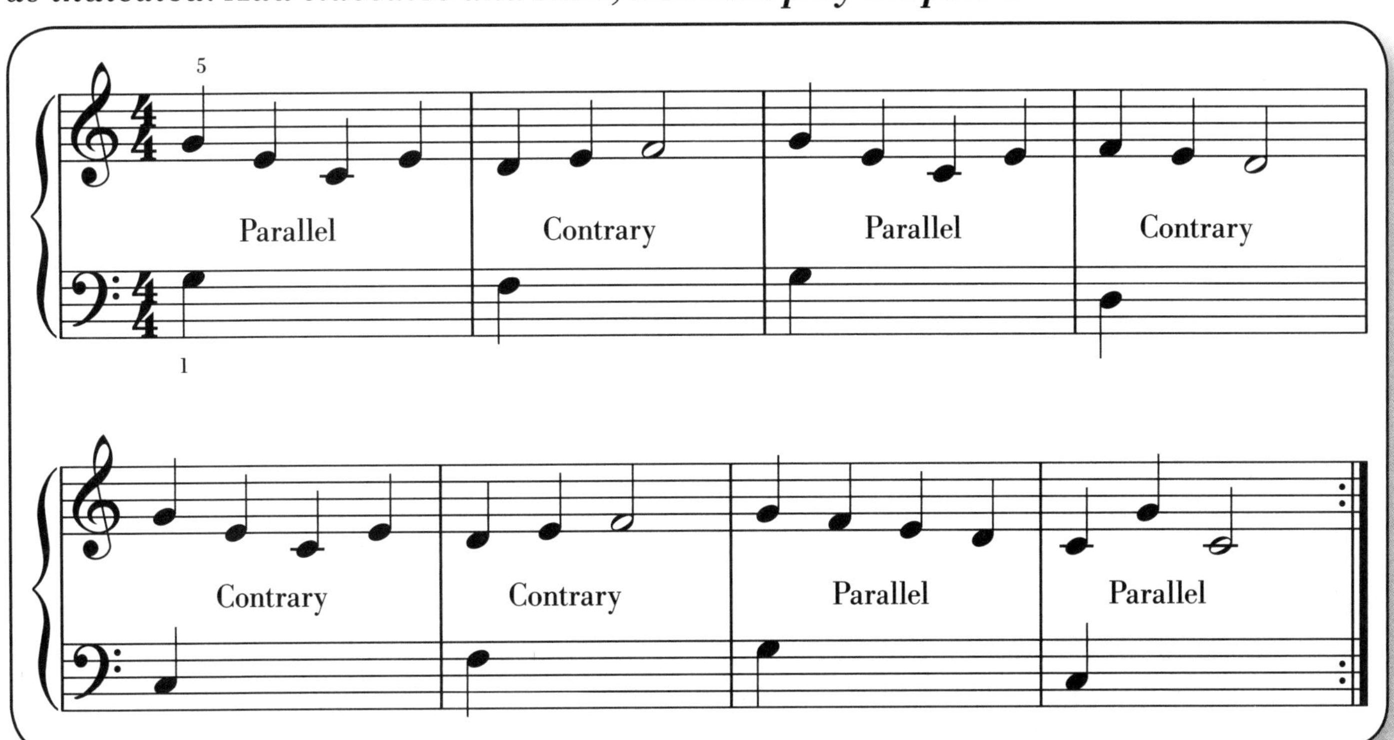

4a. Ready to Review

♫ ***Label the interval type and size below each measure. For example, a melodic second is "M2," and a harmonic fifth is "H5."***

______ ______ ______ ______ ______ ______

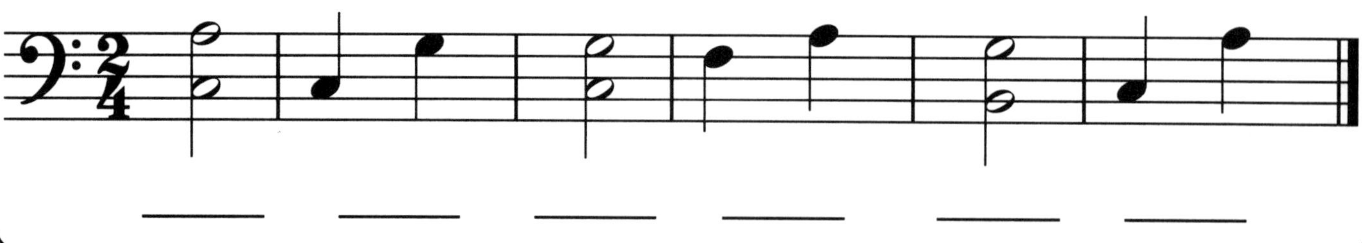

4b. Lead the Way!

C
C/E
F
G7
G/B

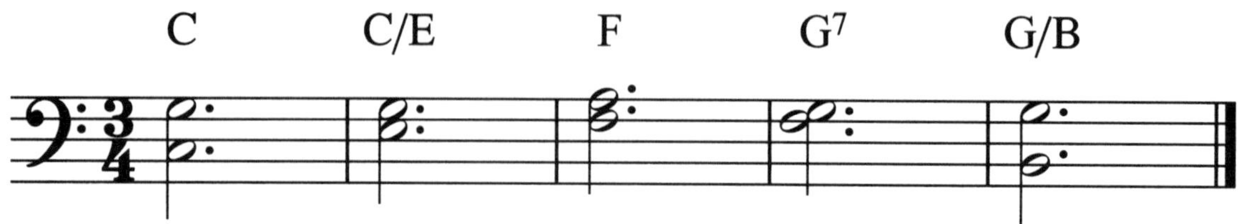

♫ ***Let's improvise a new version of*** "For He's a Jolly Good Fellow." ***Play the melody and improvise the left hand using the given chord symbols and the options above.***

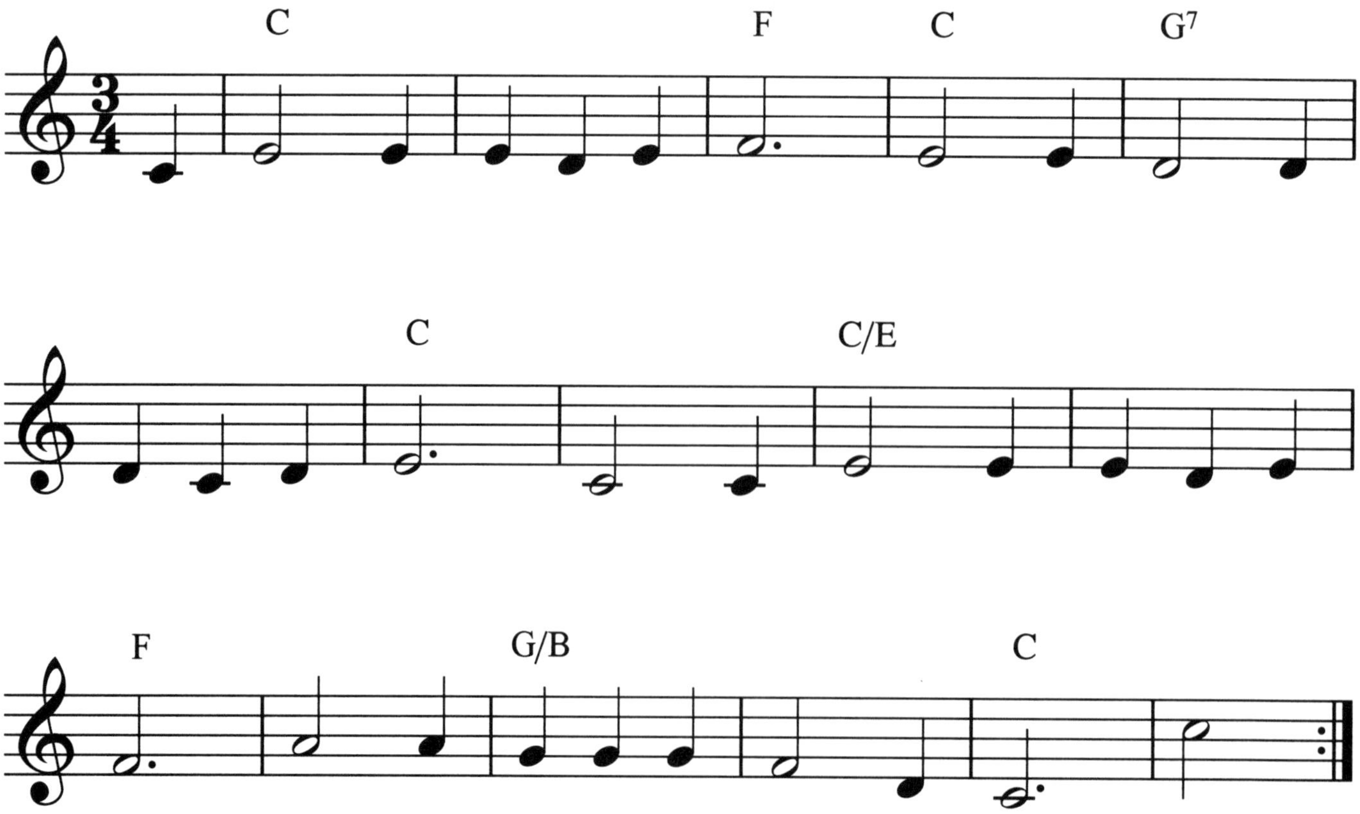

C
F
C
G7
C
C/E
F
G/B
C

4c. Power Play

♫ ***Play the examples below. Use the fingerings provided.***

EXAMPLE 1:

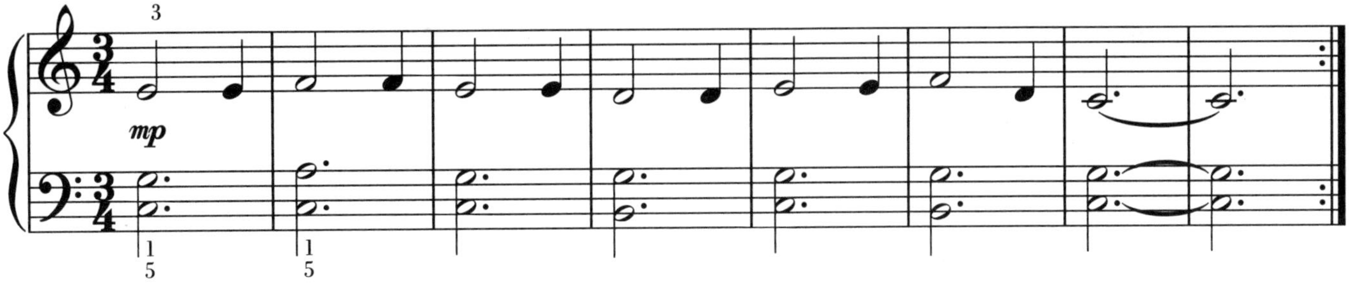

EXAMPLE 2:

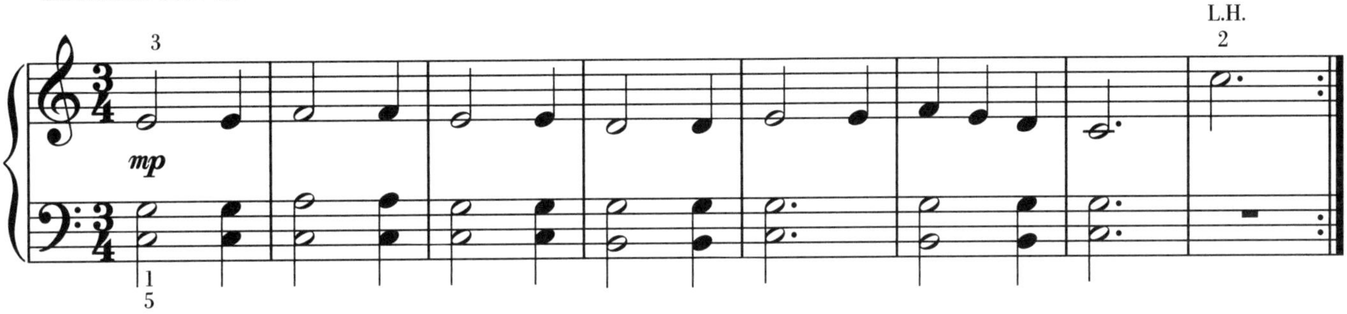

4d. I'm All Ears!

♫ ***Your teacher will play one of the examples on each line. Circle what you hear, and then identify if it is parallel or contrary motion.***

1. I hear:

____________ ____________

2. I hear:

____________ ____________

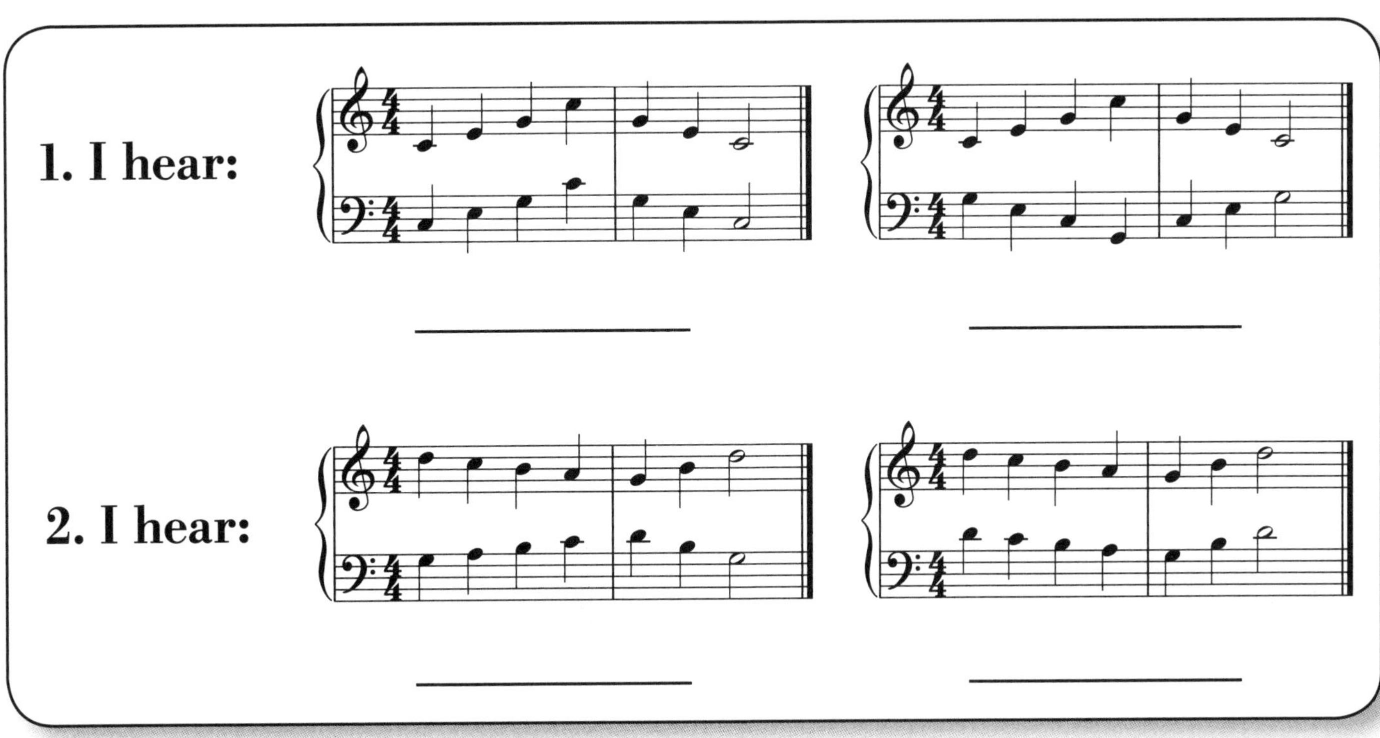

5a. Ready to Review

♫ ***Add up the beat values. Answers will be numbers.****

♩. + ♪ = ____ 𝅗𝅥. + ♩ = ____

♫ + 𝅝 = ____ 𝅗𝅥 + ♫ = ____

♫ ***Add fingerings to the examples below in the circles provided. To achieve the smoothest and most efficient fingerings, avoid using the same finger two times in a row! Play the examples using the chord symbols to improvise the left hand.***

EXAMPLE 1:

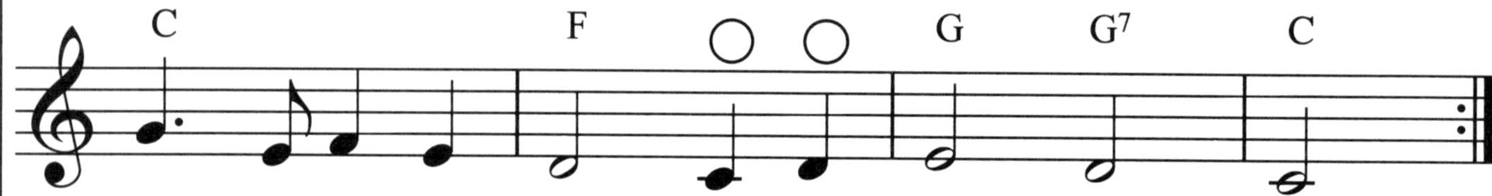

EXAMPLE 2:

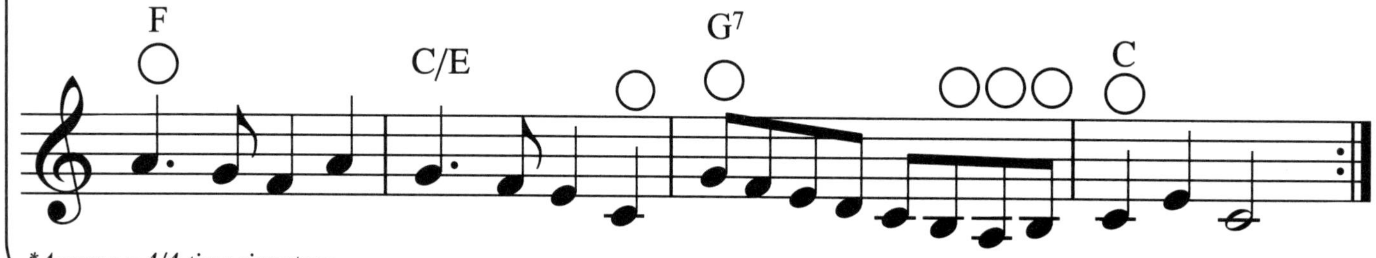

**Assume a 4/4 time signature.*

5b. Power Play

♫ ***Play the examples below. Use the fingerings provided.***

EXAMPLE 1:

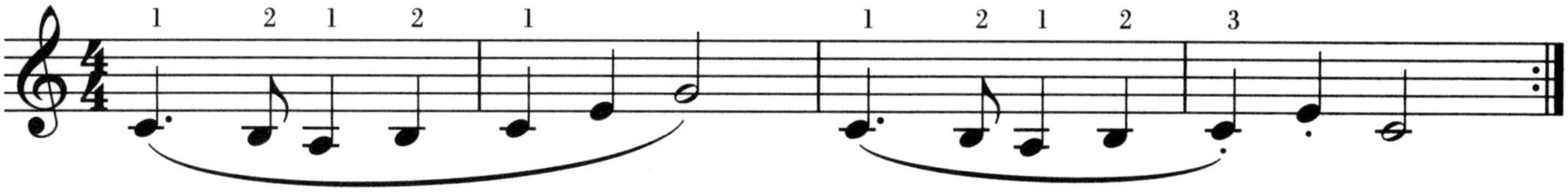

EXAMPLE 2:

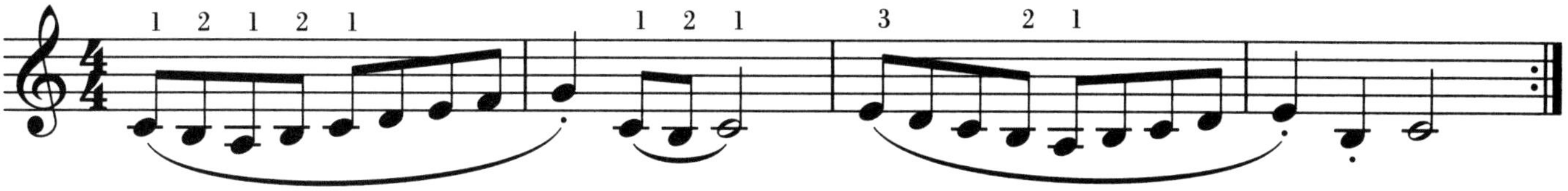

EXAMPLE 3:

5c. Composition Corner

♫ ***Copy the notes from measures 1-3 into measures 5-7. Add fingerings and chord symbols. Play the piece when you are done.***

6a. Ready to Review

♫ *Add an accent mark below each note with a stem going up.*

♫ *Add an accent mark above each note with a stem going down.*

6b. Analyze This

♫ *Follow the directions to analyze and complete the piece below.*

1. How many slurs can you find? _____ How many ties? _____
2. How many staccatos can you find? _____ How many accent marks? _____
3. Notate the bass clef notes according to the chord symbols. Play the piece.

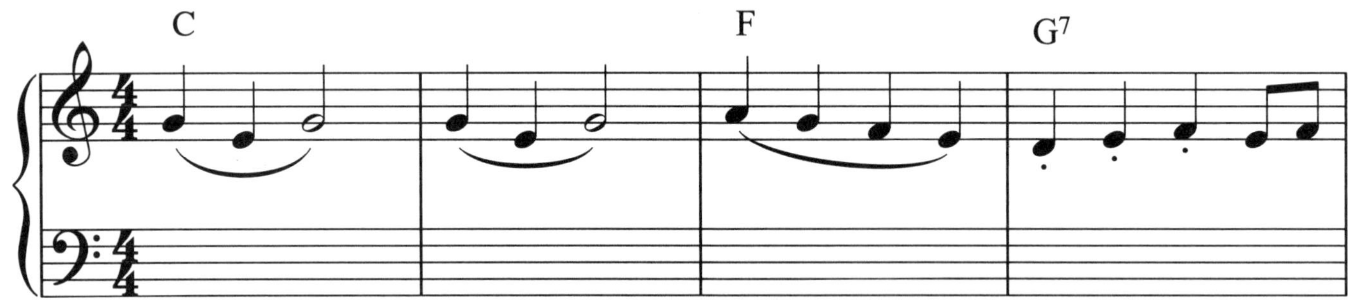

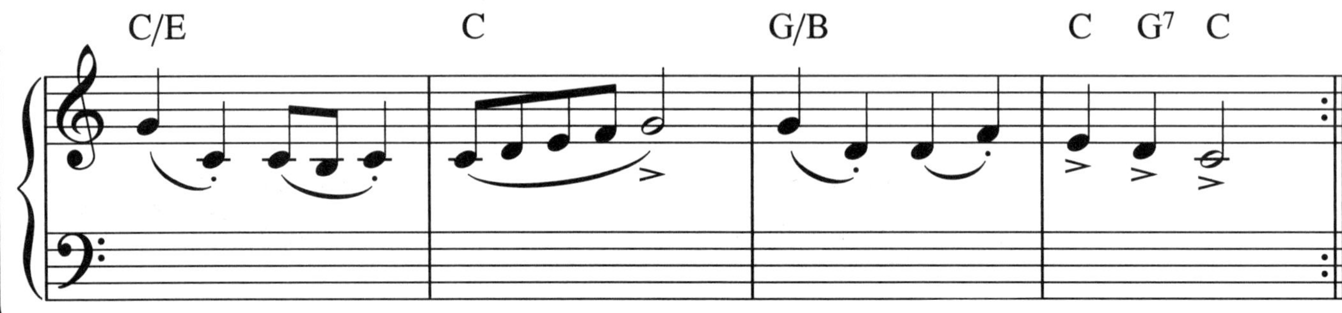

6c. Power Play

♫ ***Play the examples below. Use the fingerings provided.***

EXAMPLE 1:

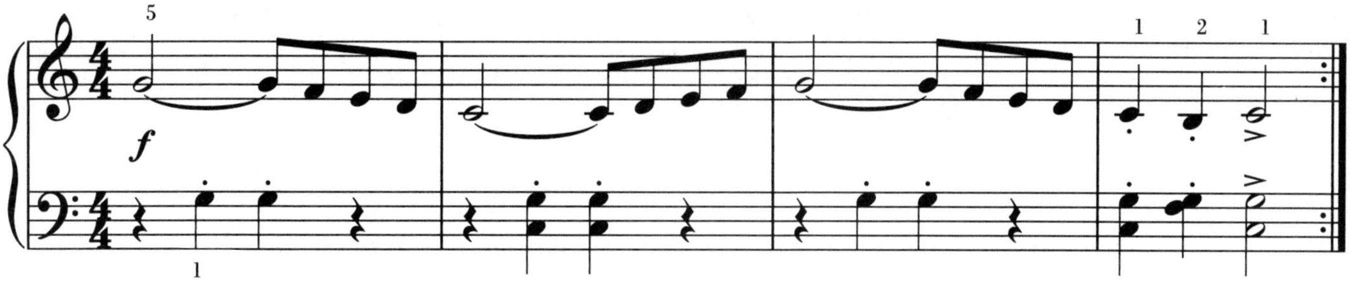

EXAMPLE 2:

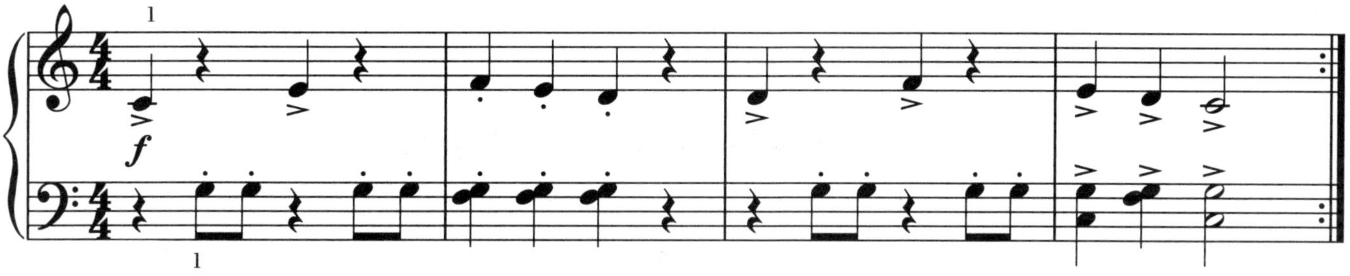

6d. I'm All Ears!

♫ ***Your teacher will play an example from each line. Circle what you hear.***

1. I hear:

2. I hear:

3. I hear:

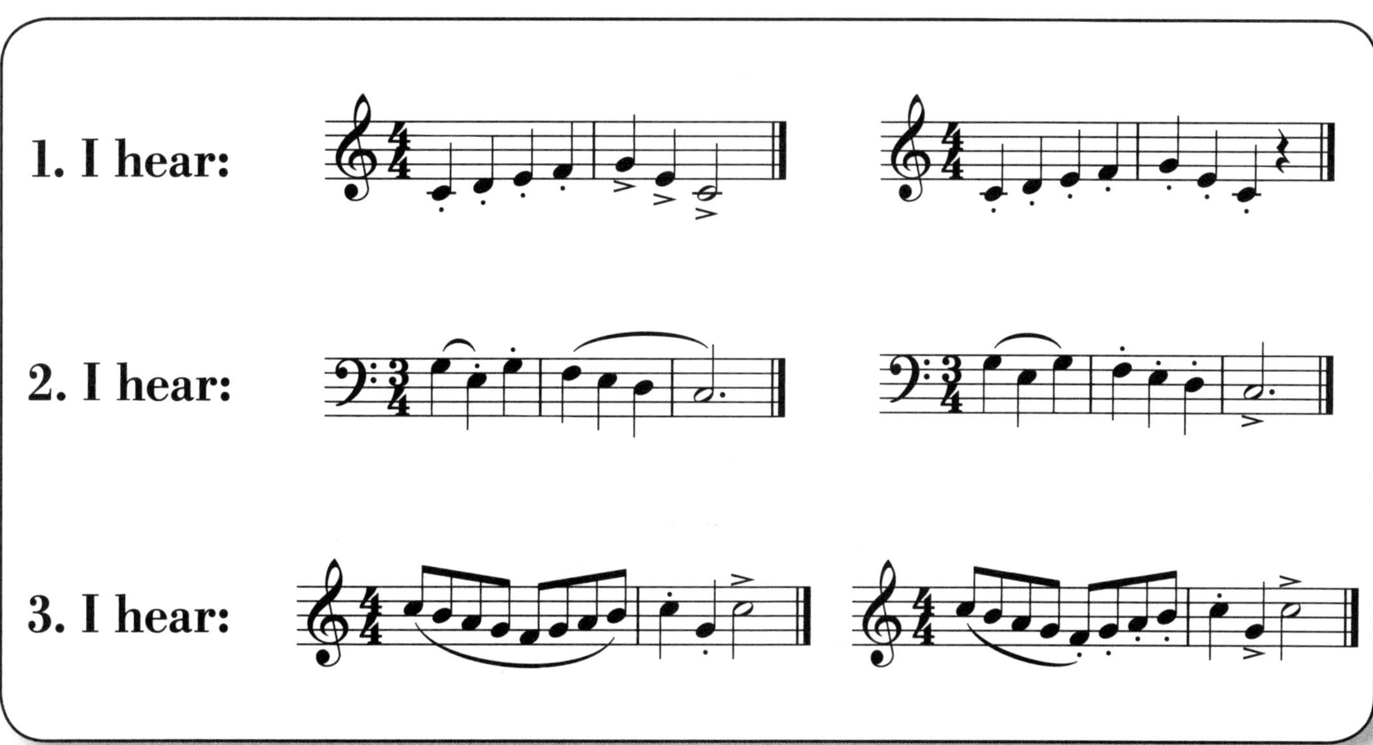

7a. Ready to Review

Write the correct beat value under each rhythm below.*

**Assume a 4/4 time signature.*

7b. Write It Right

Follow the directions complete the piece below.

1. Draw a repeat sign at the end of measure 8.
2. Draw a final barline at the end of measure 10.
3. Add a first ending bracket above measures 7 and 8.
4. Add a second ending bracket above measures 9 and 10.
5. Notate the bass clef notes according to the chord symbols.
6. Play the piece.

7c. Power Play

♫ ***Play the examples below. Use the fingerings provided.***

EXAMPLE 1:

EXAMPLE 2:

7d. Ahead of Schedule

♫ ***Find and play the left-hand F-sharp that you will use in the next piece.***

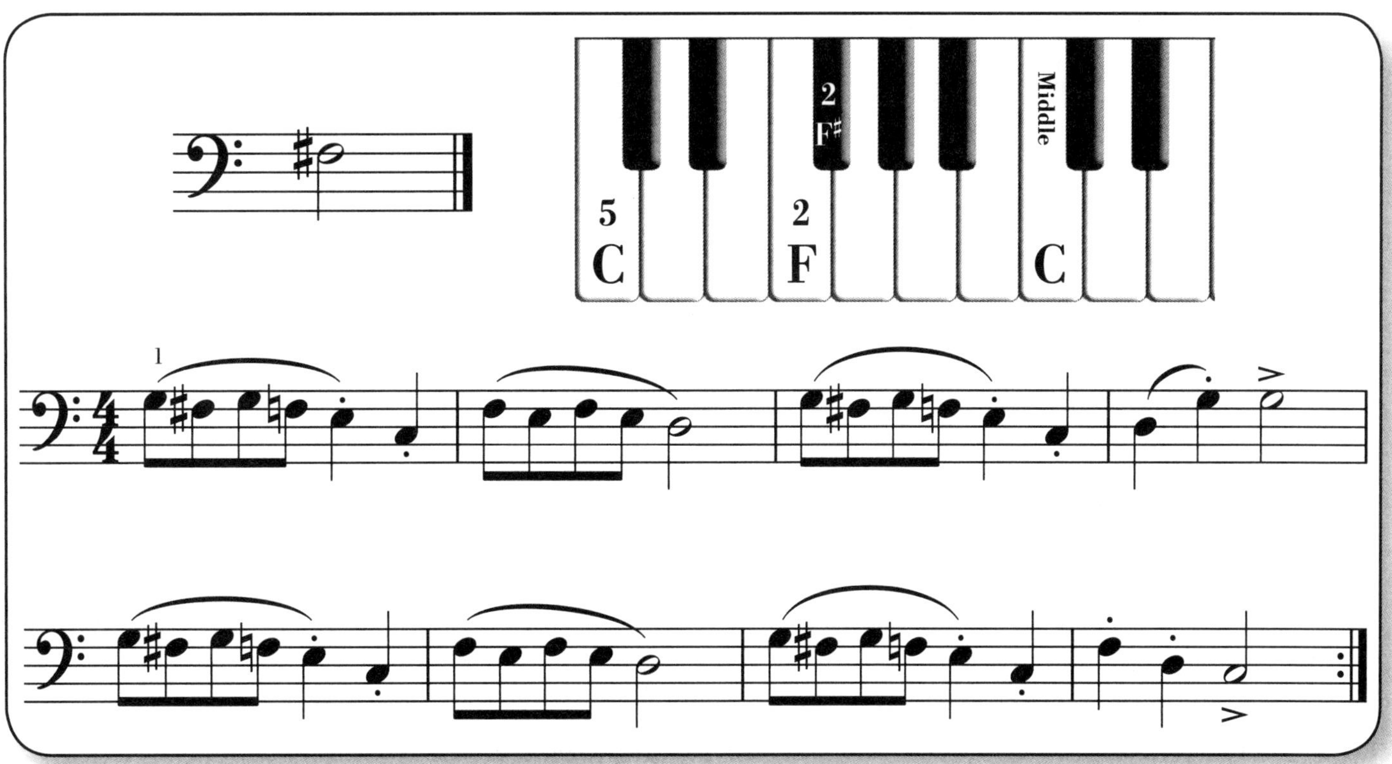

8a. Ready to Review

♫ ***Label the note names between the staves. Each measure will spell a word.***

♫ ***Name the numbered keys as sharps in the spaces provided. You can write your answer in words or symbols. Remember: Accidentals are not always black keys!***

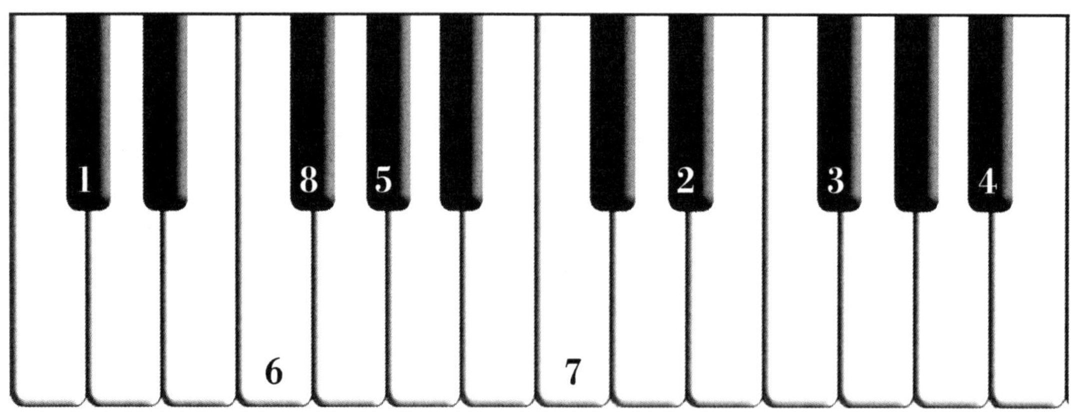

1. ____________
2. ____________
3. ____________
4. ____________
5. ____________
6. ____________
7. ____________
8. ____________

8b. Power Play

♫ ***Play the examples below. Use the fingerings provided.***

EXAMPLE 1:

EXAMPLE 2:

EXAMPLE 3:

8c. Composition Corner

♫ ***Add chord symbols to harmonize the melody. Add fingerings and play the piece.***

9a. Ready to Review

♫ ***Draw the correct interval size and type according to the instructions. The arrow indicates whether the interval should be above or below the given note.***

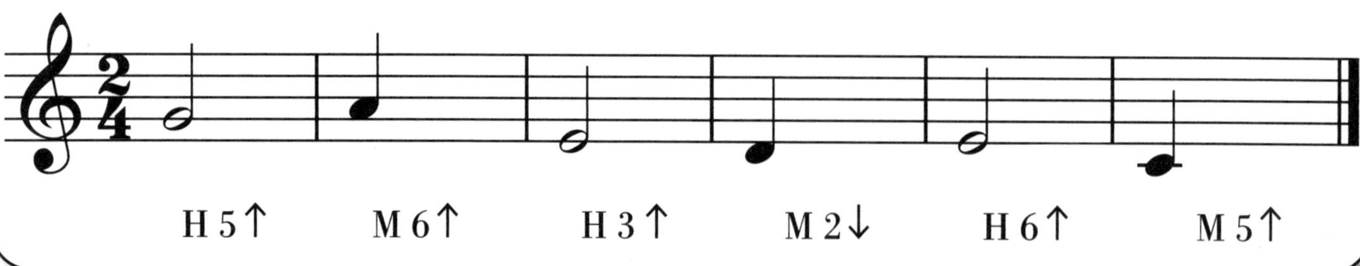

9b. Strong & Weak Beats

Each time signature has a natural pattern in which certain beats are lightly accented, though not marked with accents. In 4/4 time, the first and third beats are strong, and the second and fourth beats are weak (unaccented). The first beat of the measure, also known as the **downbeat**, is the strongest beat of the measure. Play the measures below. (S=strong; W=weak)

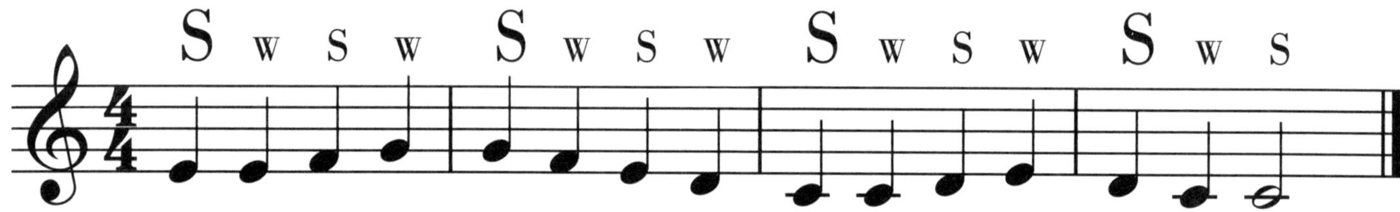

♫ ***Harmonize the melody using the chord symbols. Place the left-hand notes on the weak beats. Add staccato marks to the notes you added, and then play the piece.***

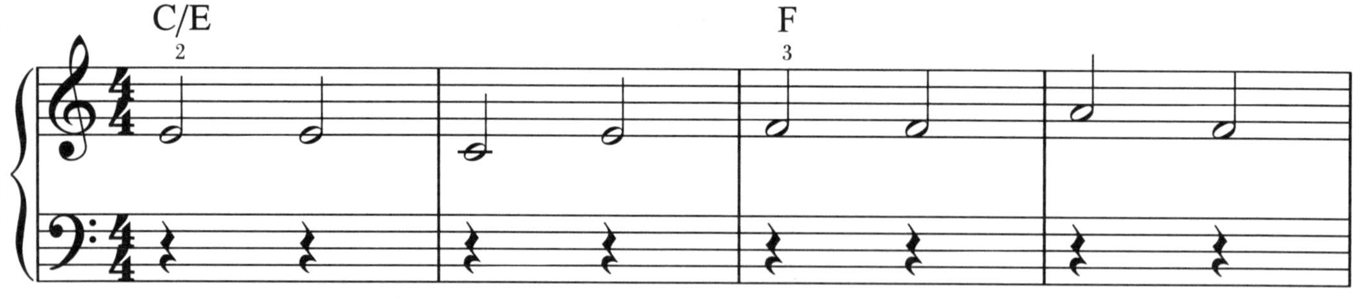

9c. Power Play

♫ ***Play the examples below. Use the fingerings provided.***

EXAMPLE 1:

EXAMPLE 2:

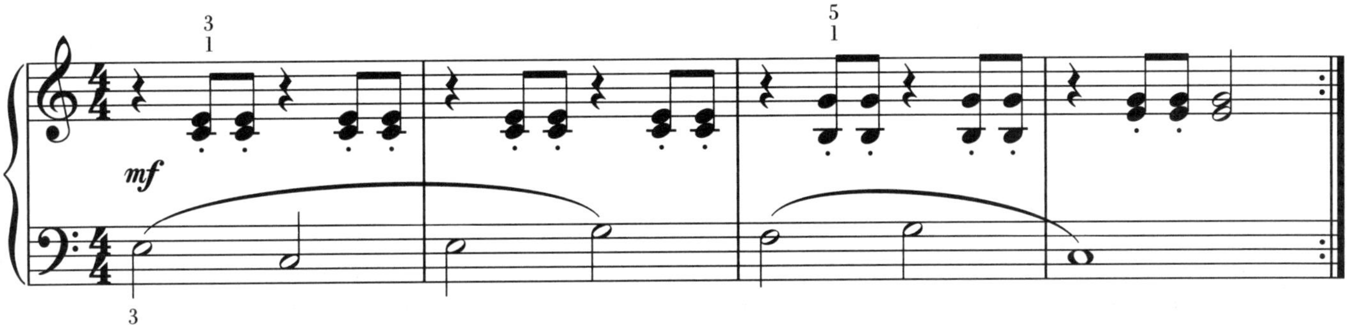

9d. Composition Corner

♫ ***Copy the notes from measures 1–3 into measures 5–7. Harmonize the melody by adding chord symbols. Play the piece, striking the left-hand chords on the weak beats.****

**Final chord plays on beat 1.*

10a. Ready to Review

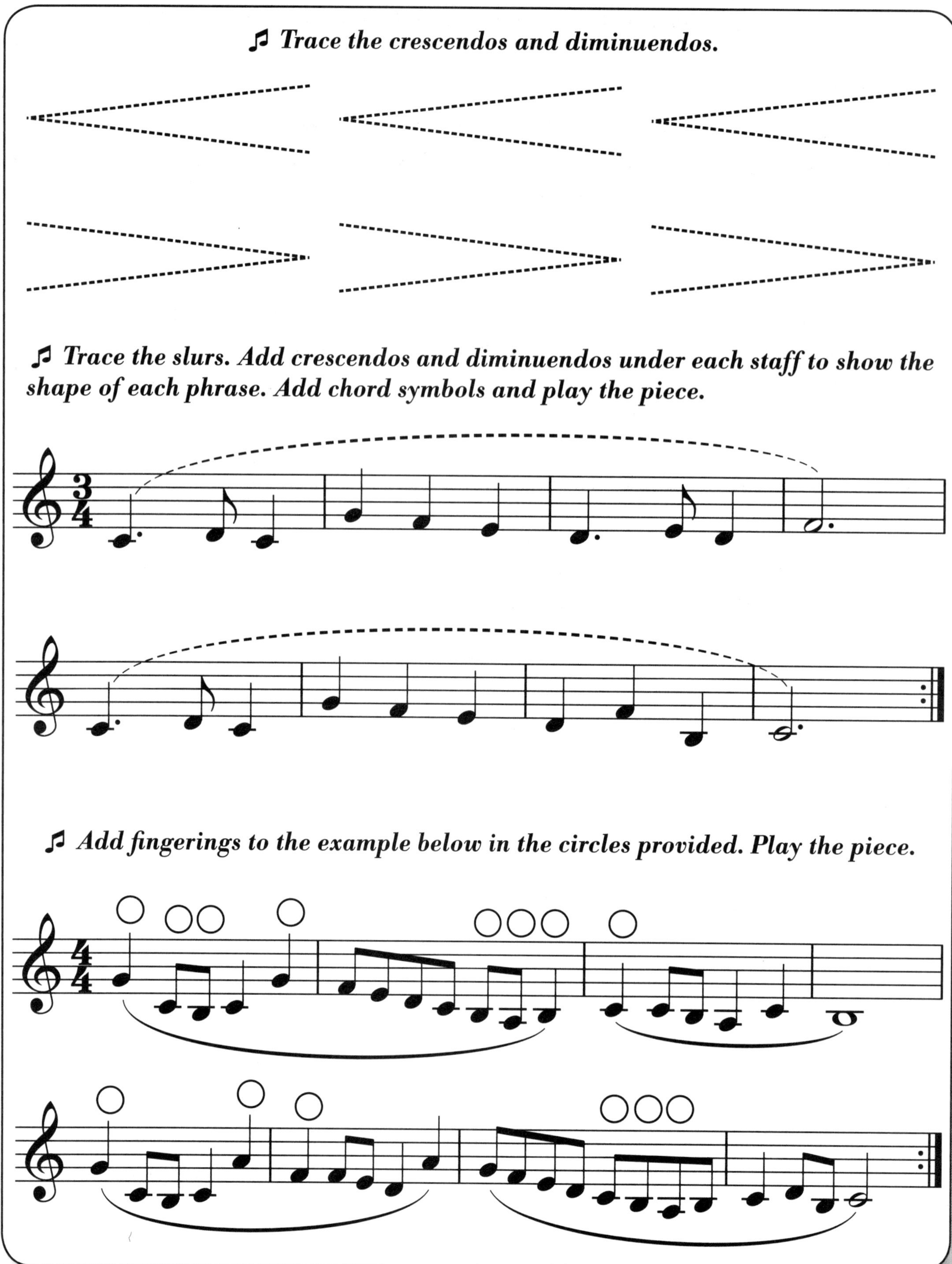

10b. Power Play

♫ *Play the examples below. In the third example, improvise the left-hand chords.*

EXAMPLE 1:

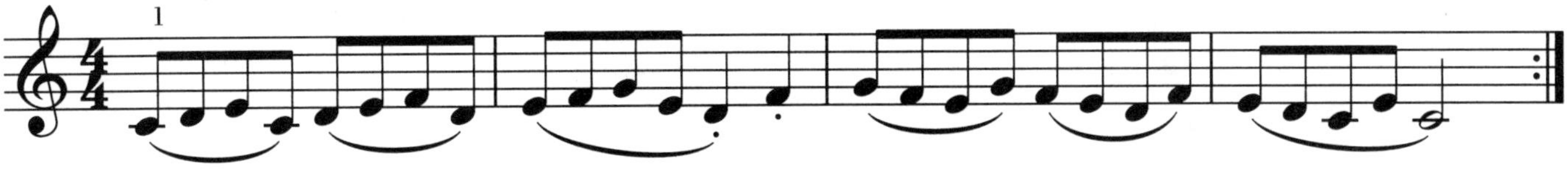

EXAMPLE 2:

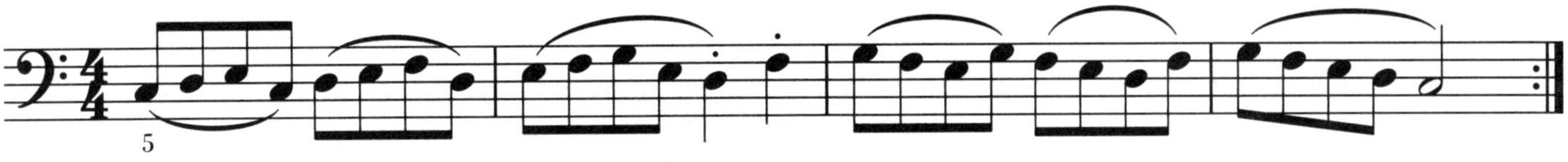

EXAMPLE 3:

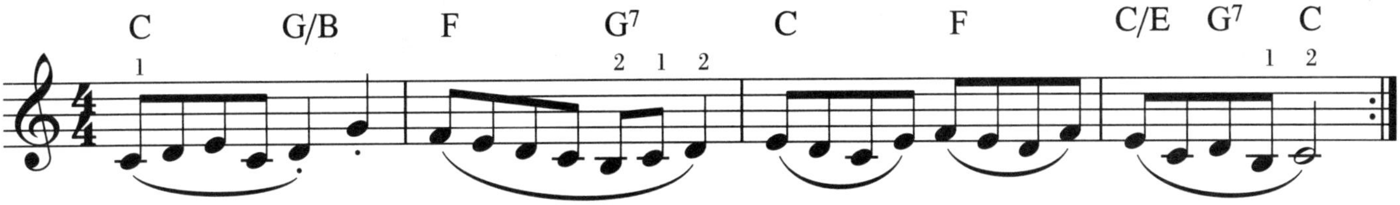

C
G/B
F
G7
C
F
C/E
G7
C

10c. Ahead of Schedule

♫ *Play the example below, which introduces the new eighth rest.*

𝄾 Eighth rest = ½ beat of silence

mf

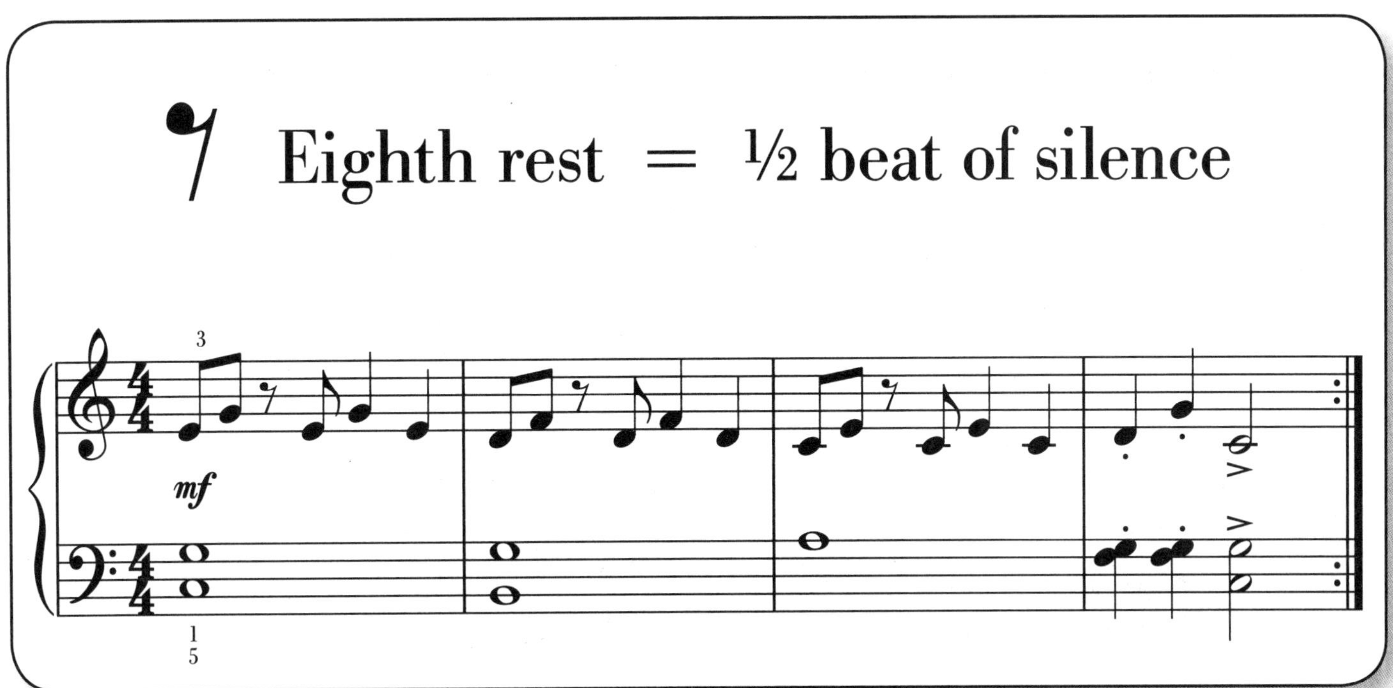

11a. Ready to Review

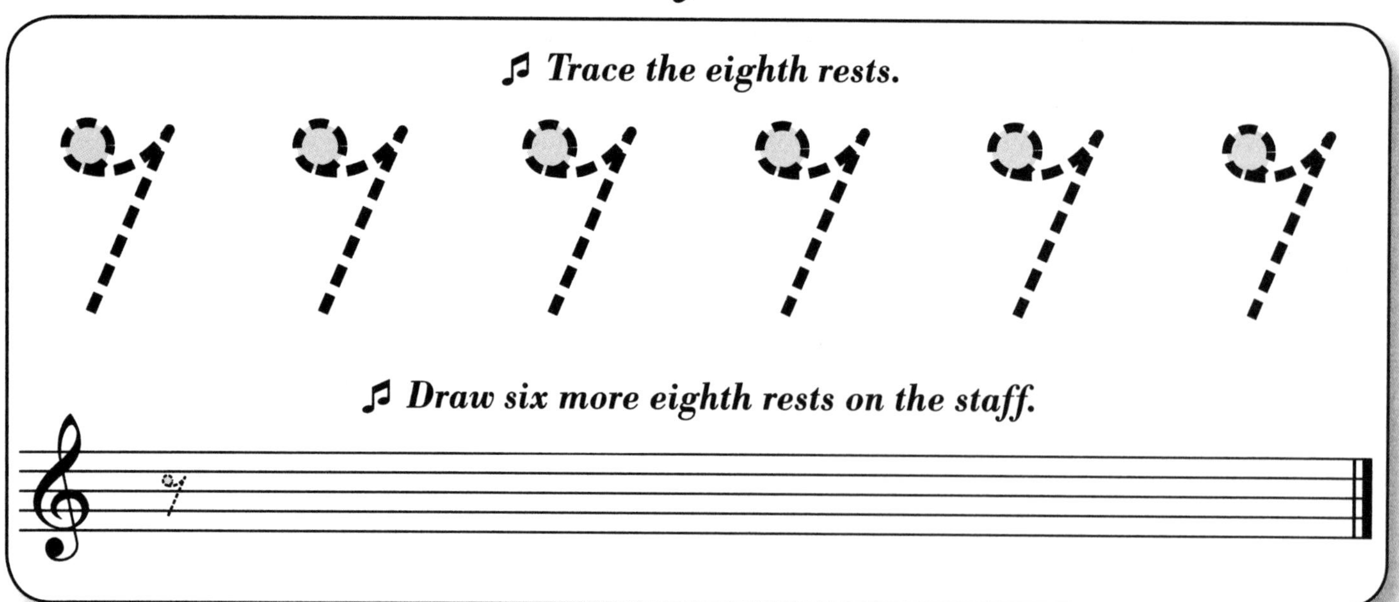

♫ ***Trace the eighth rests.***

♫ ***Draw six more eighth rests on the staff.***

11b. Lead the Way!

C
F
F/C
G7
G/B

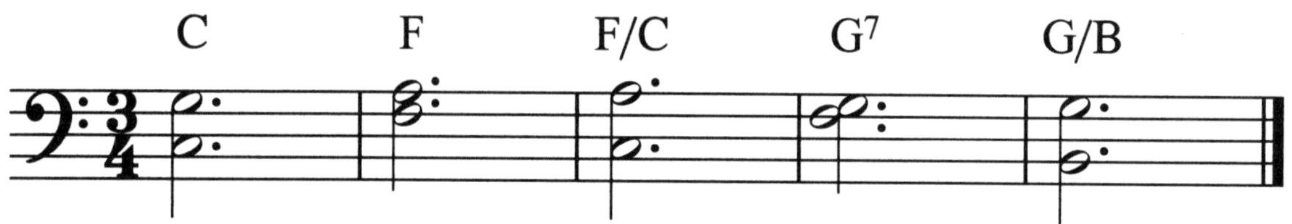

♫ ***Play the melody and improvise the left hand.***

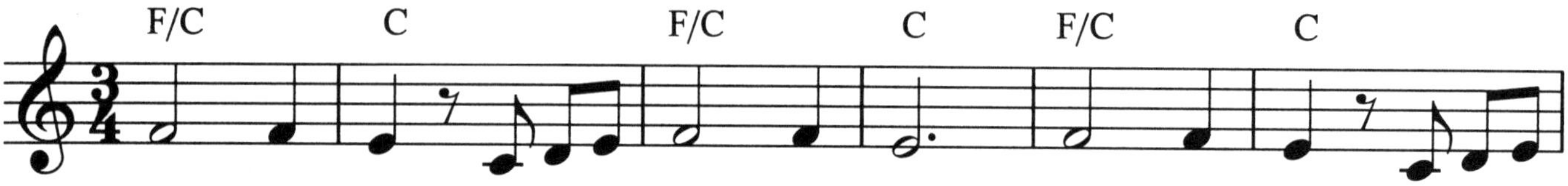

F/C
C
F/C
C
F/C
C

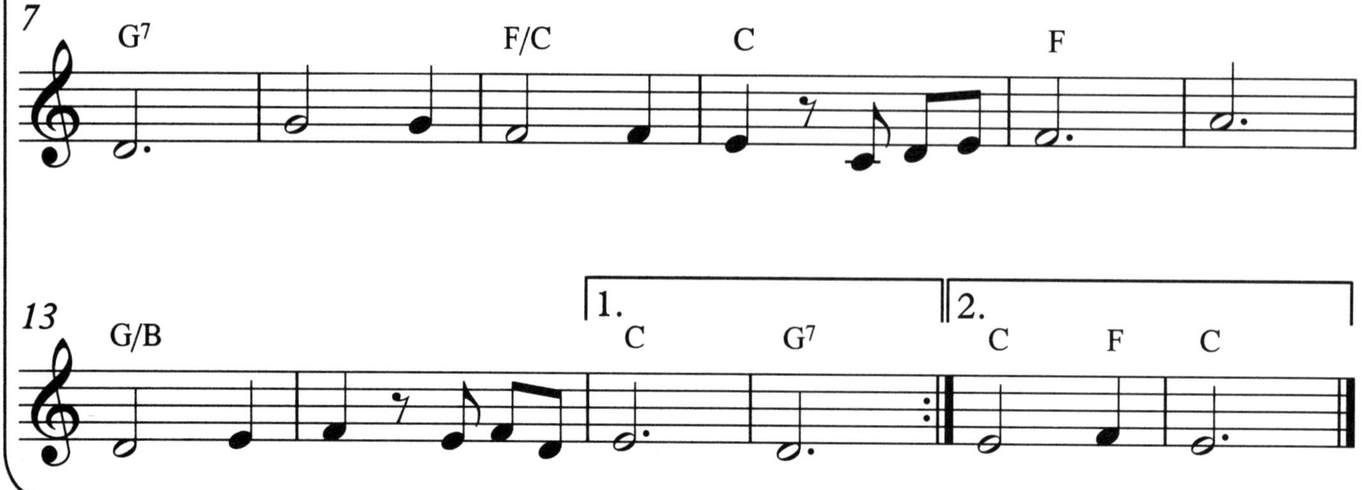

7
G7
F/C
C
F
13
G/B
1.
C
G7
2.
C
F
C

11c. Power Play

♫ ***Play the examples below. Use the fingerings provided.***

EXAMPLE 1:

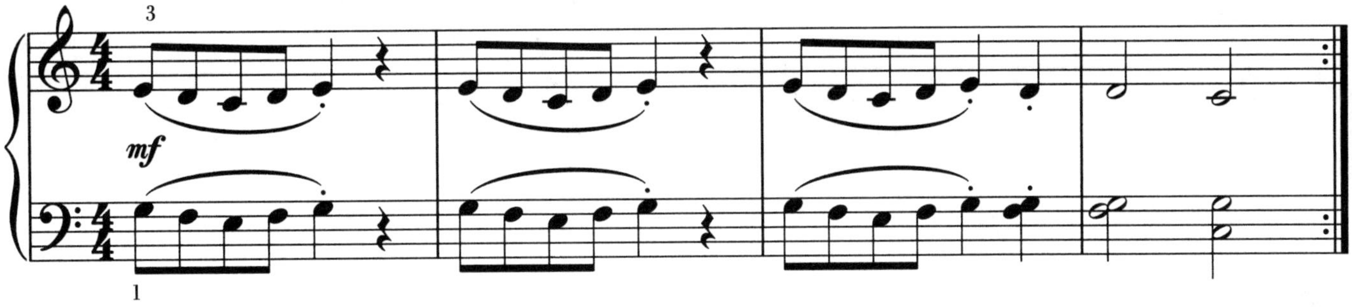

EXAMPLE 2:

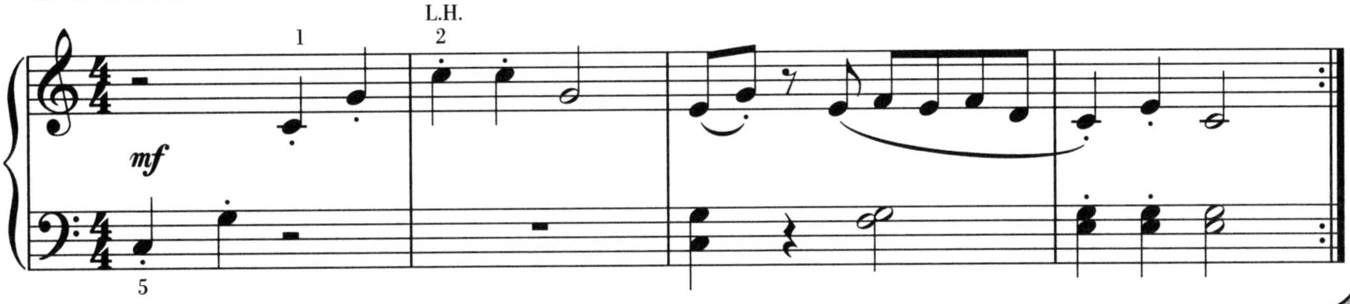

11d. I'm All Ears!

♫ ***Your teacher will play one example from each line. Circle what you hear.***

1. I hear:

2. I hear:

3. I hear:

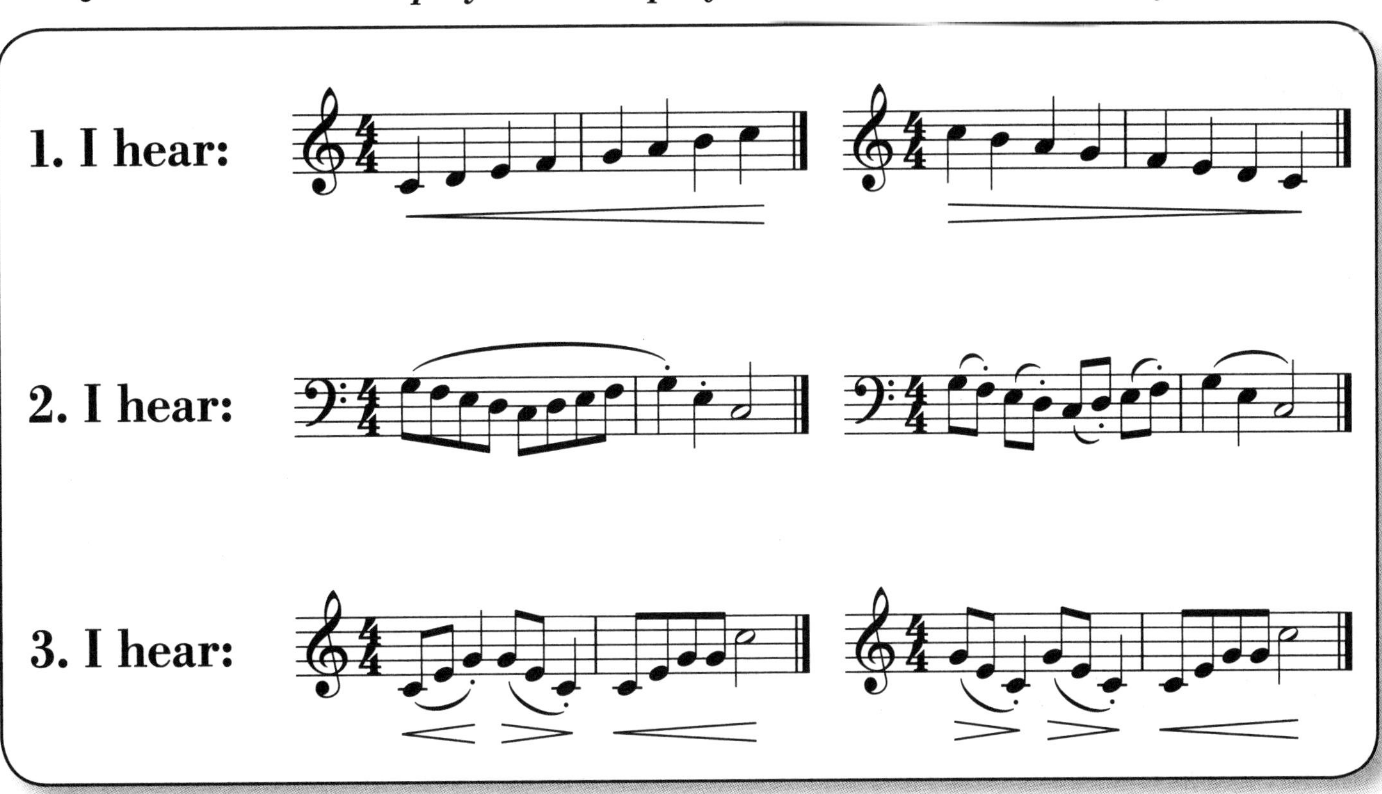

12a. Ready to Review

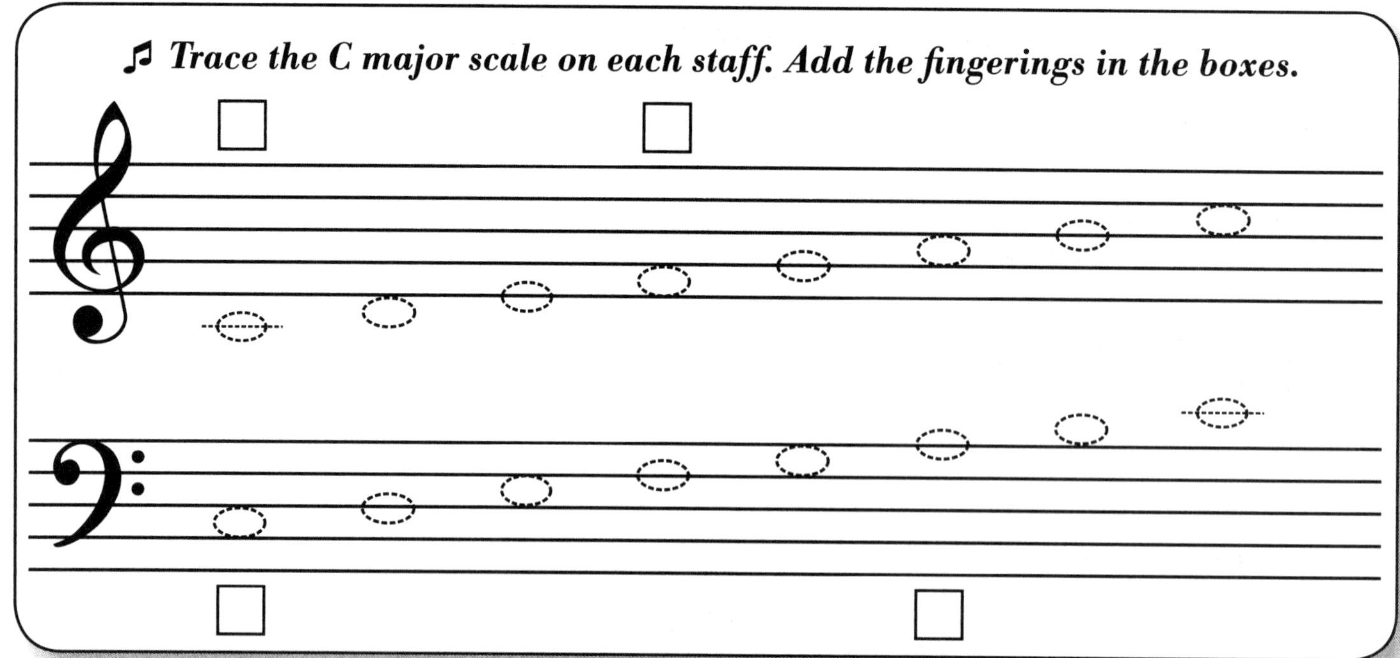

12b. Chords & Triads

Chord = three or more notes sounded together. Chords may have different intervals between all of the notes. Two notes sounded together can also be called a chord or a **harmonic interval**.

Triad = a three-note chord, stacked in thirds, and sounded together. On the staff: line-line-line or space-space-space. (Hint: a triad looks like three scoops of ice cream.)

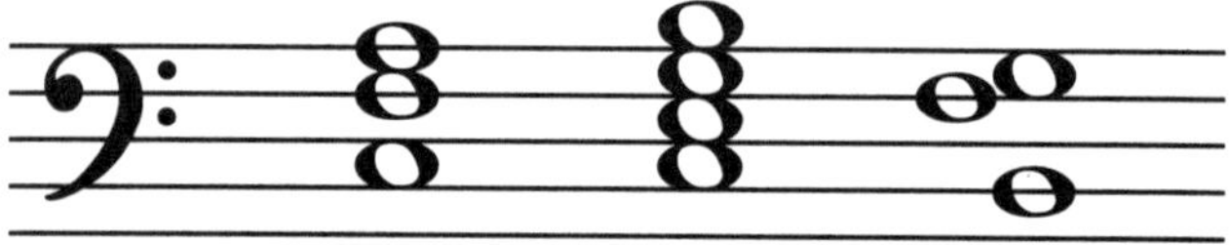

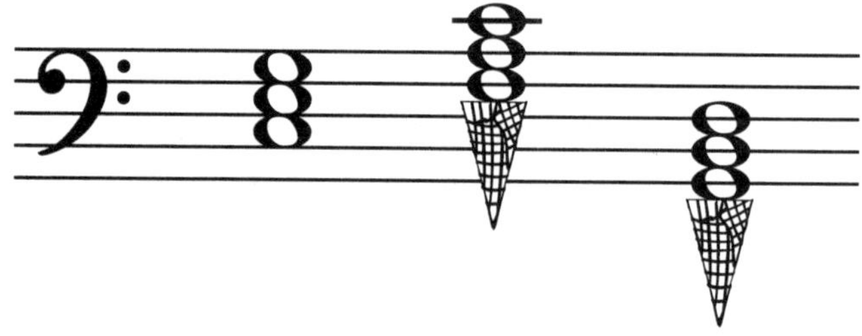

Triad root or **chord root** = the note on which the triad is built (the bottom note).

♫ *Build triads above each given root. Color the triad root your favorite color.*

12c. Power Play

♫ ***Let's practice playing the C major scale in contrary motion with both hands.****

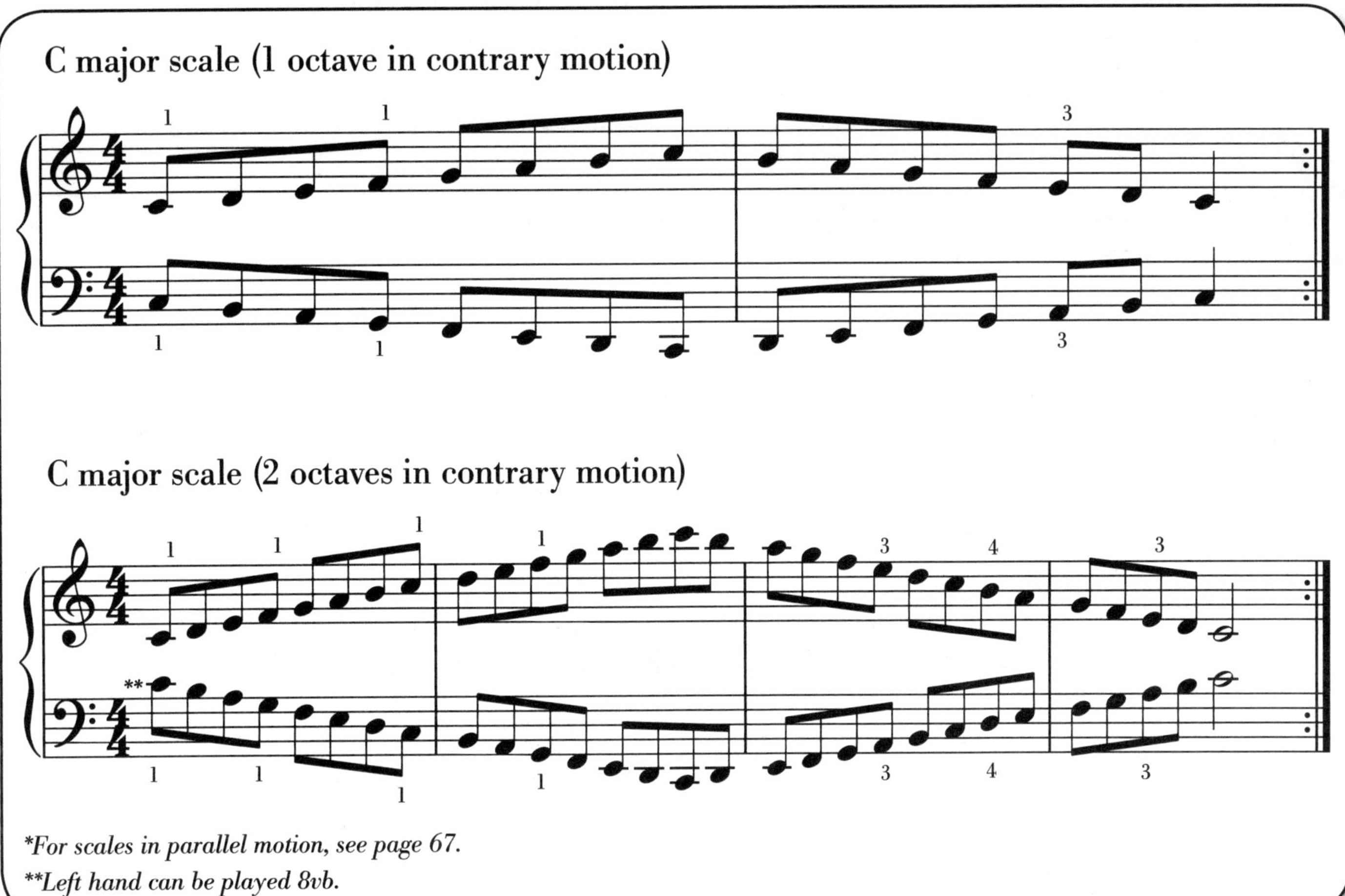

**For scales in parallel motion, see page 67.*

***Left hand can be played 8vb.*

12d. I'm All Ears!

Major = bright, cheerful sounds **Minor** = dark, melancholy sounds

♫ ***Your teacher will play a major or minor triad. Circle what you hear.***

1. I hear a: **major triad** ***or*** **minor triad**

2. I hear a: **major triad** ***or*** **minor triad**

3. I hear a: **major triad** ***or*** **minor triad**

4. I hear a: **major triad** ***or*** **minor triad**

5. I hear a: **major triad** ***or*** **minor triad**

13a. Ready to Review

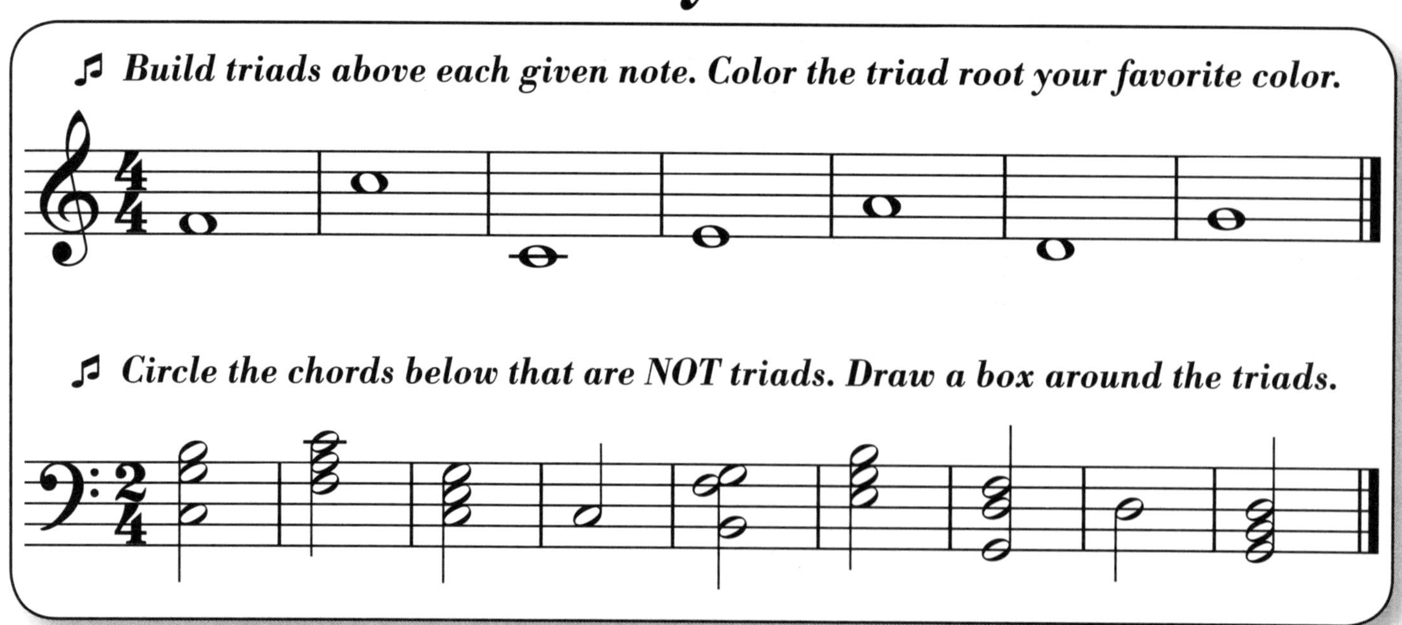

13b. Minor & Major 2nds

Intervals consist of two parts: **number** and **quality**. The number refers to how many letter names or staff positions the interval encompasses. Both the beginning and ending notes are included in the count. The quality can be perfect (P), major (M), minor (m), augmented (A), or diminished (d) and is determined by how many half steps are present in the interval.

Minor 2nd (m2)

On the piano = a half step

On the staff = line to space; space to line

Major 2nd (M2)

On the piano = a whole step

On the staff = line to space; space to line

♫ ***Label each interval as a minor second (m2) or a major second (M2). Use the piano to help count the half steps.***

13c. Power Play

♫ *Play the examples below. Use the fingerings provided.*

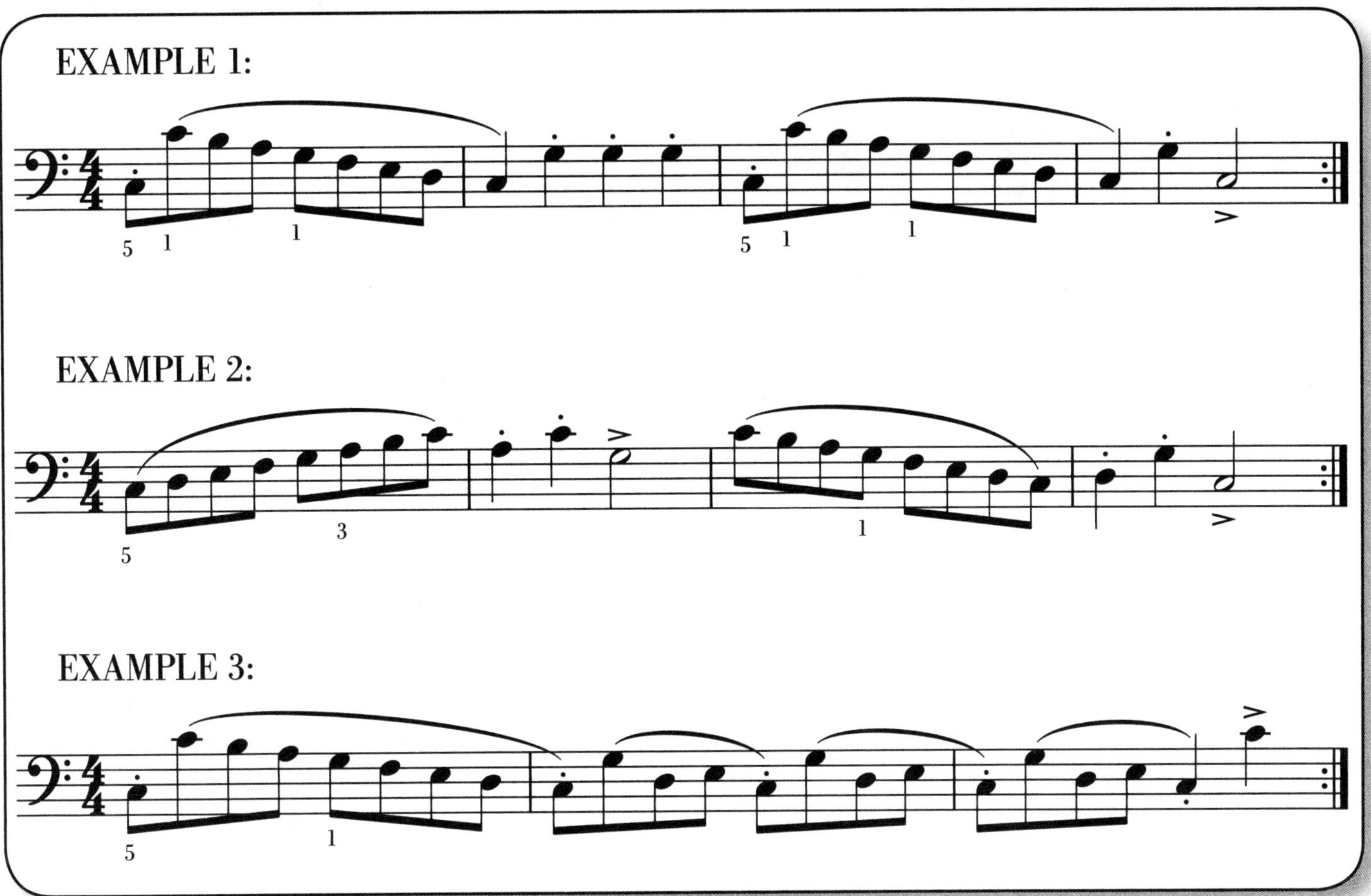

13d. I'm All Ears!

♫ *Your teacher will play one of the examples below.* Circle what you hear.*

1. I hear a:	**chord**	***or***	**melodic interval**
2. I hear a:	**major triad**	***or***	**minor triad**
3. I hear a:	**major triad**	***or***	**minor triad**
4. I hear a:	**minor 2nd**	***or***	**major 3rd**
5. I hear a:	**major 2nd**	***or***	**major 3rd**
6. I hear a:	**major 2nd**	***or***	**minor 2nd**

**Play intervals harmonically, unless otherwise noted. Use consonance and dissonance to help differentiate 2nds and 3rds.*

14a. Intervals: 4ths

The left-hand D–G combination you played in *Non più andrai* is an example of a **fourth (4th)**. Study the examples below to learn how to build fourths on the white keys and on the staff.

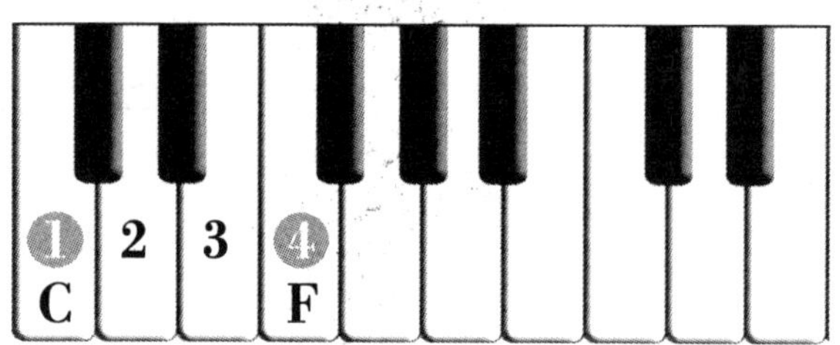

Start from any white key and count that as number one. Count every white key up (or down) to find the fourth white key.

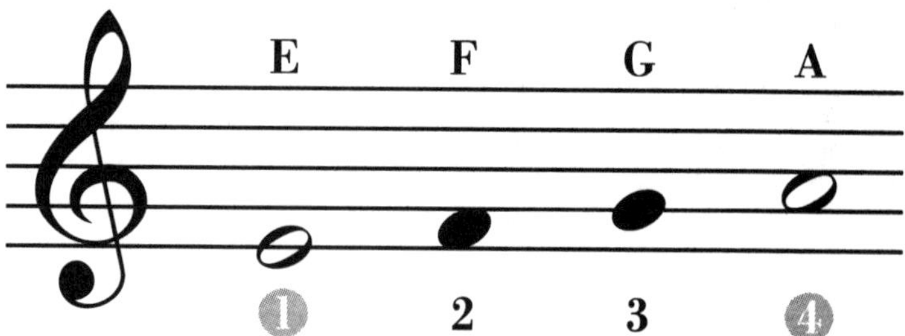

To draw a fourth on the staff, count the starting note as number one. Count up (or down) each line and space to find the fourth. E to A is a fourth.

♫ ***Complete each measure by drawing a half note a fourth ABOVE the given note.***

14b. Perfect Intervals

Perfect intervals are considered to have perfect consonance, meaning they do not sound as if they need to resolve to another chord. Unisons and octaves are always perfect, as are most fourths and fifths. Study the staff below to see examples of perfect intervals.

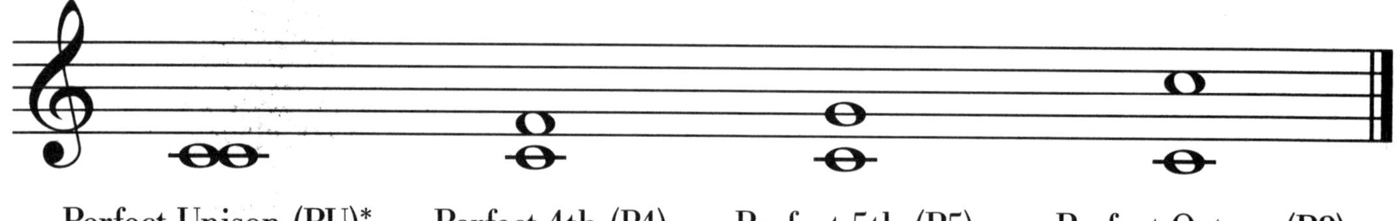

Perfect Unison (PU)*	Perfect 4th (P4)	Perfect 5th (P5)	Perfect Octave (P8)
Same note	*5 half steps*	*7 half steps*	*Same note 8 keys up/down*

♫ ***Label each perfect interval below as a PU, P4, P5, or P8.***

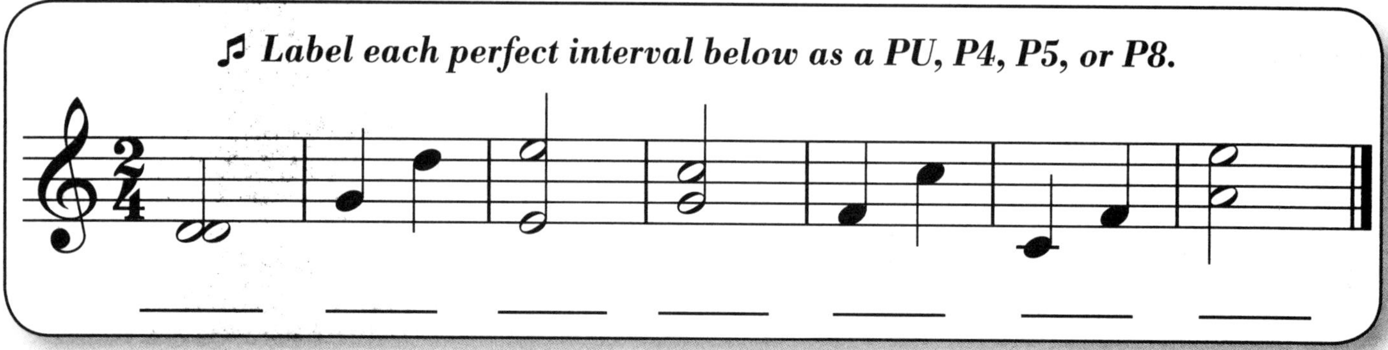

**Note: Perfect unisons can also be labeled as "P1."*

14c. Power Play

♫ *Play the examples below. Use the fingerings provided.*

EXAMPLE 1:

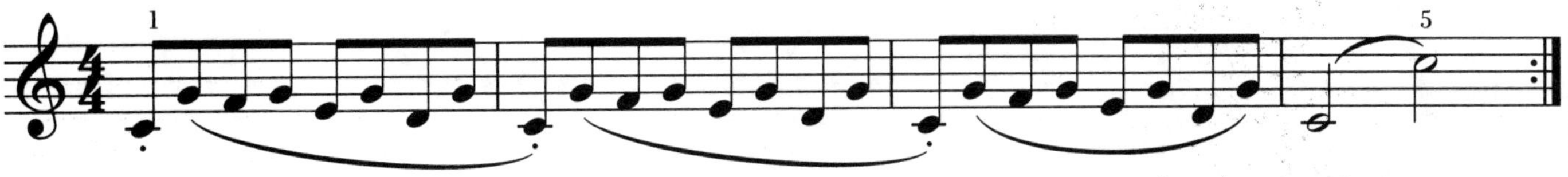

EXAMPLE 2:

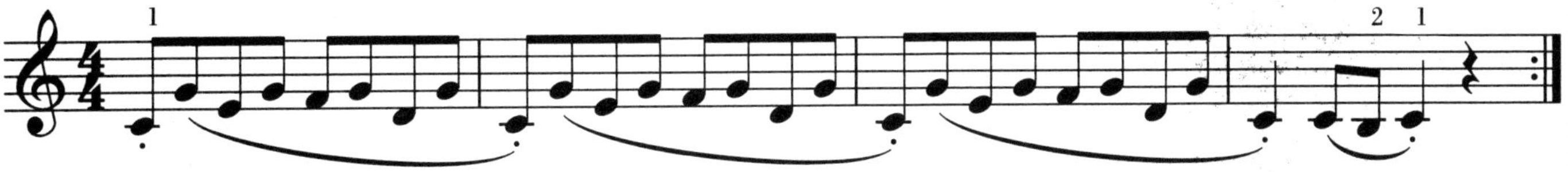

EXAMPLE 3:

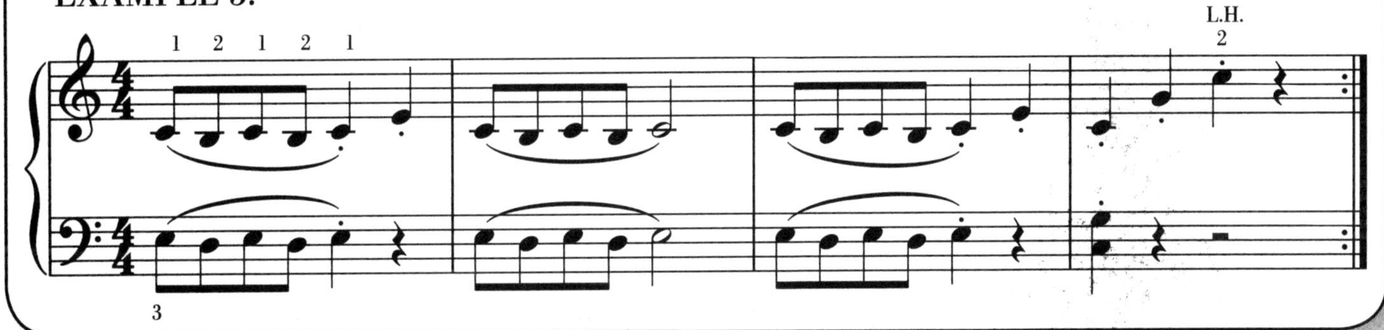

L.H.

14d. I'm All Ears!

♫ ***Your teacher will play the second note of each melodic interval above or below the given note in each example. Complete the measure to notate what you hear.***

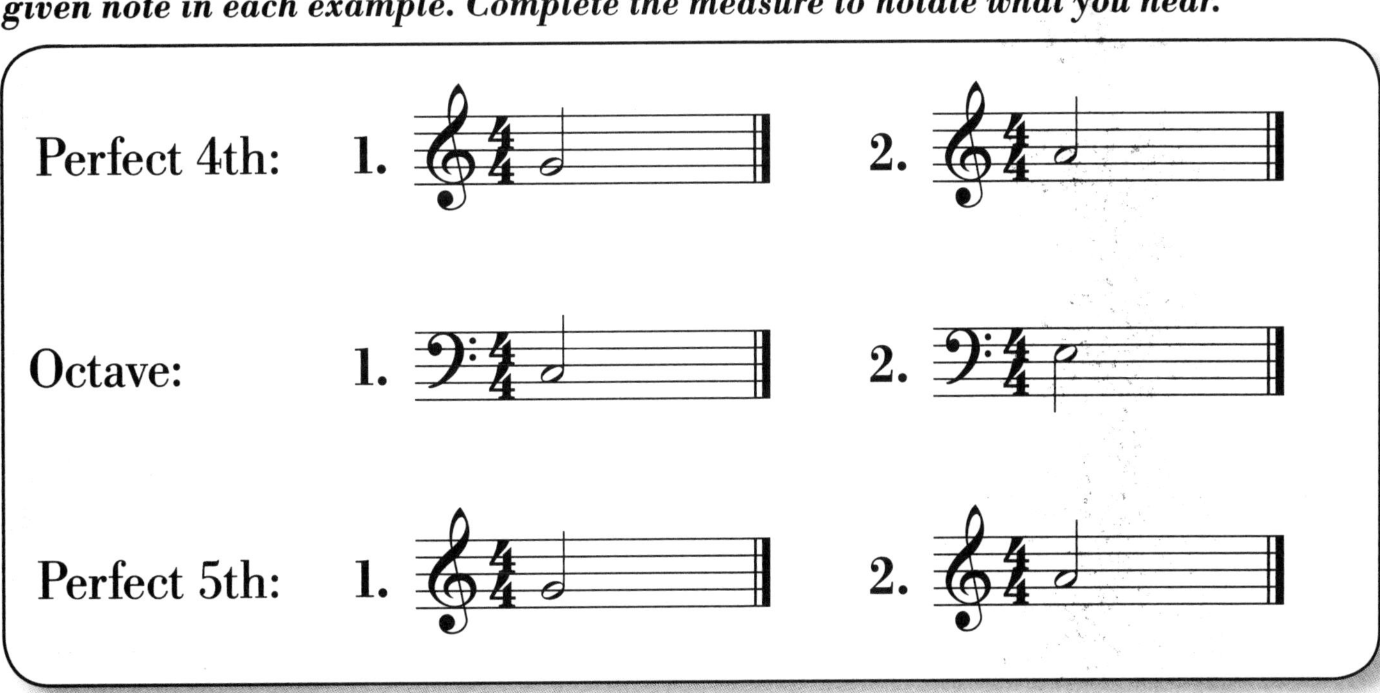

15a. Ready to Review

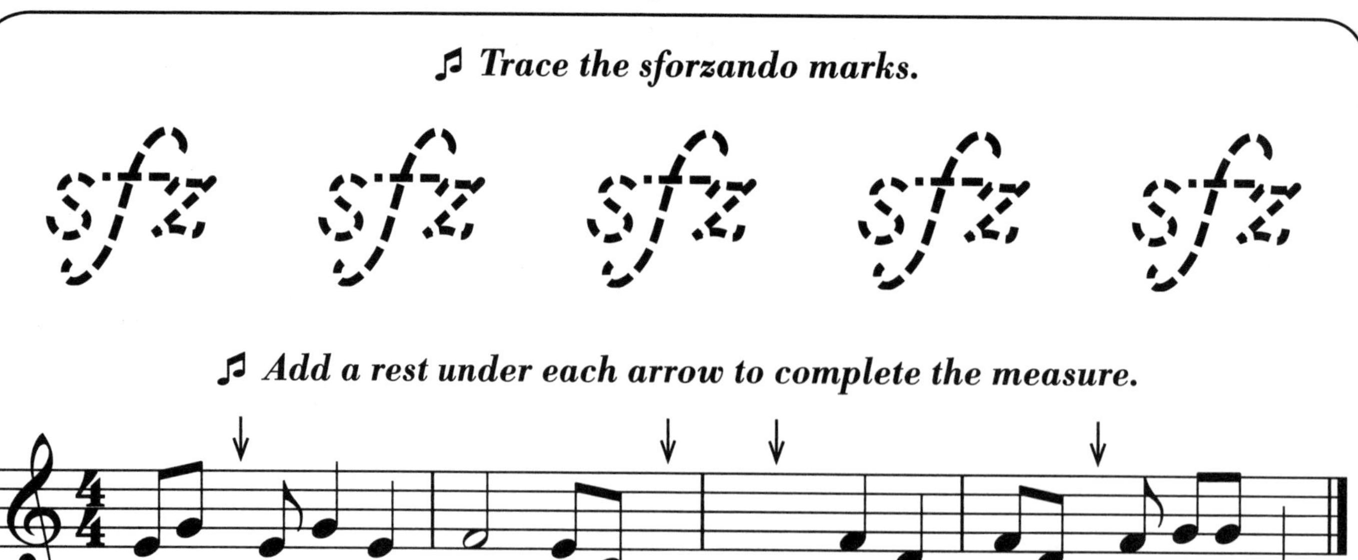

15b. Minor & Major 3rds

Minor 3rd (m3)

On the piano = 3 half steps
On the staff = line to line; space to space

Major 3rd (M3)

On the piano = 4 half steps
On the staff = line to line; space to space

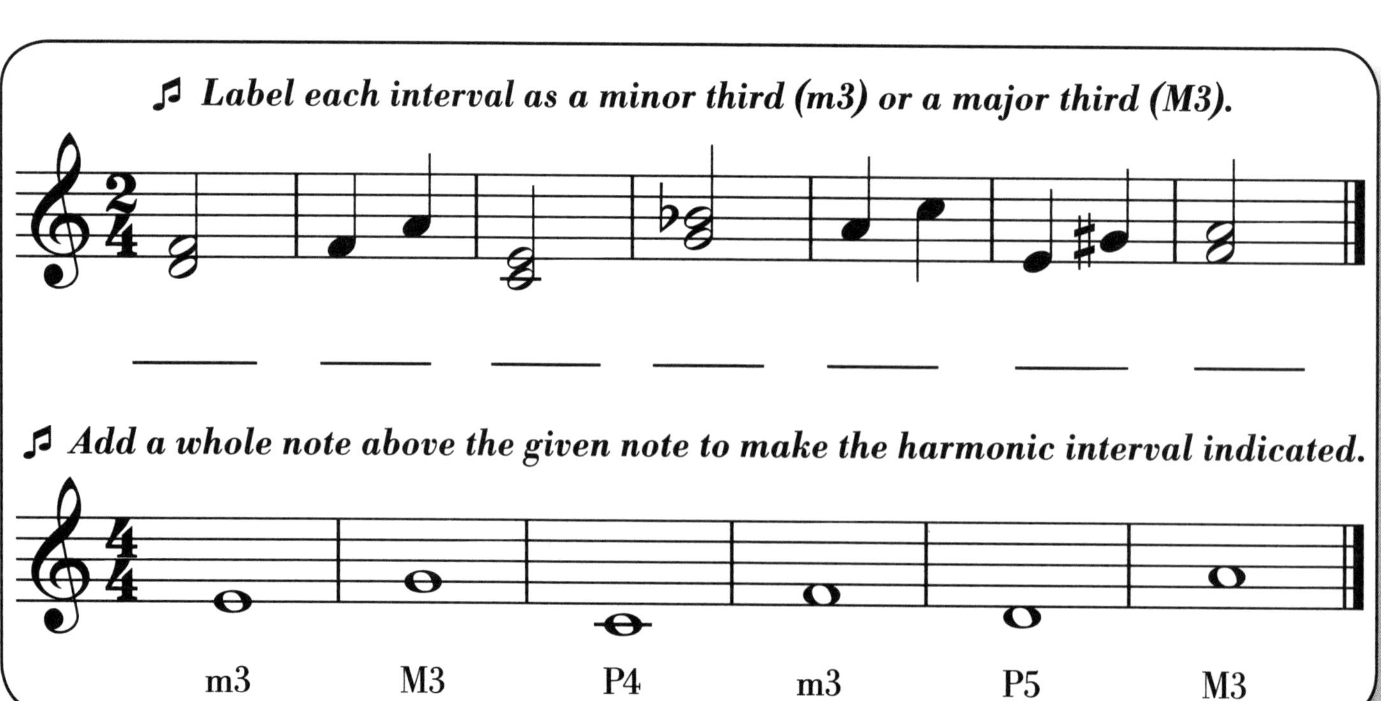

15c. Power Play

♫ ***Play the examples below. Use the fingerings provided.***

EXAMPLE 1:

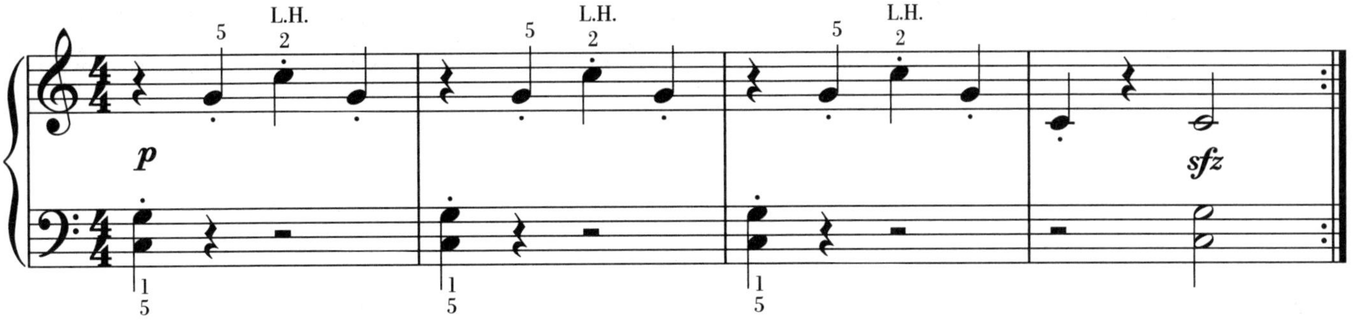

EXAMPLE 2:

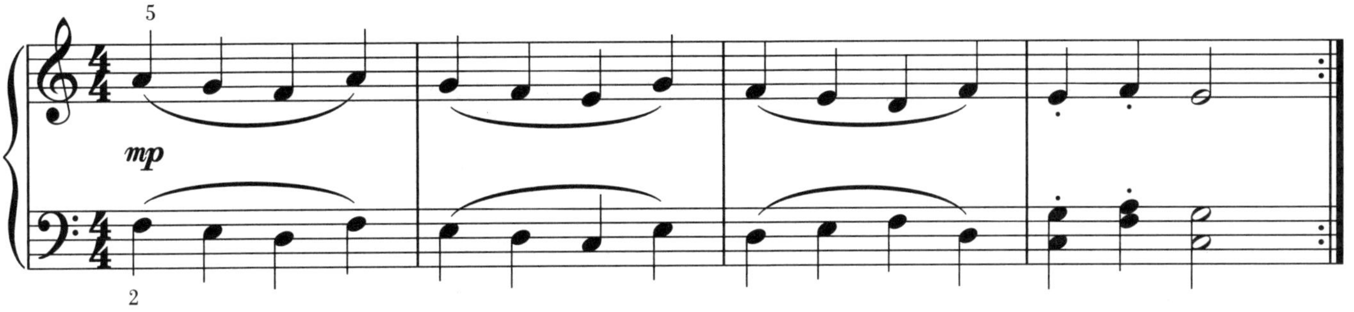

15d. Composition Corner

♫ ***Compose measures 5–7 and add chord symbols to all measures. Add a tempo marking and a title. Play the piece.***

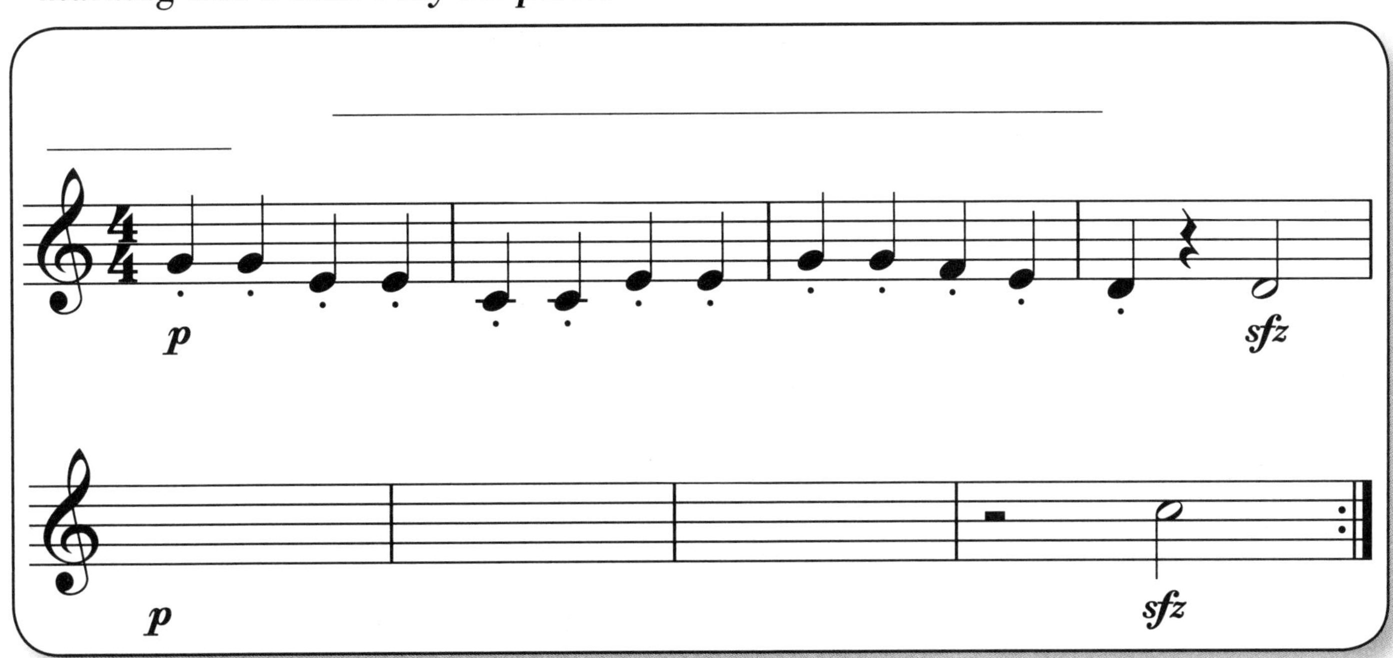

16a. Ready to Review

♫ ***Label the notes in the spaces provided.***

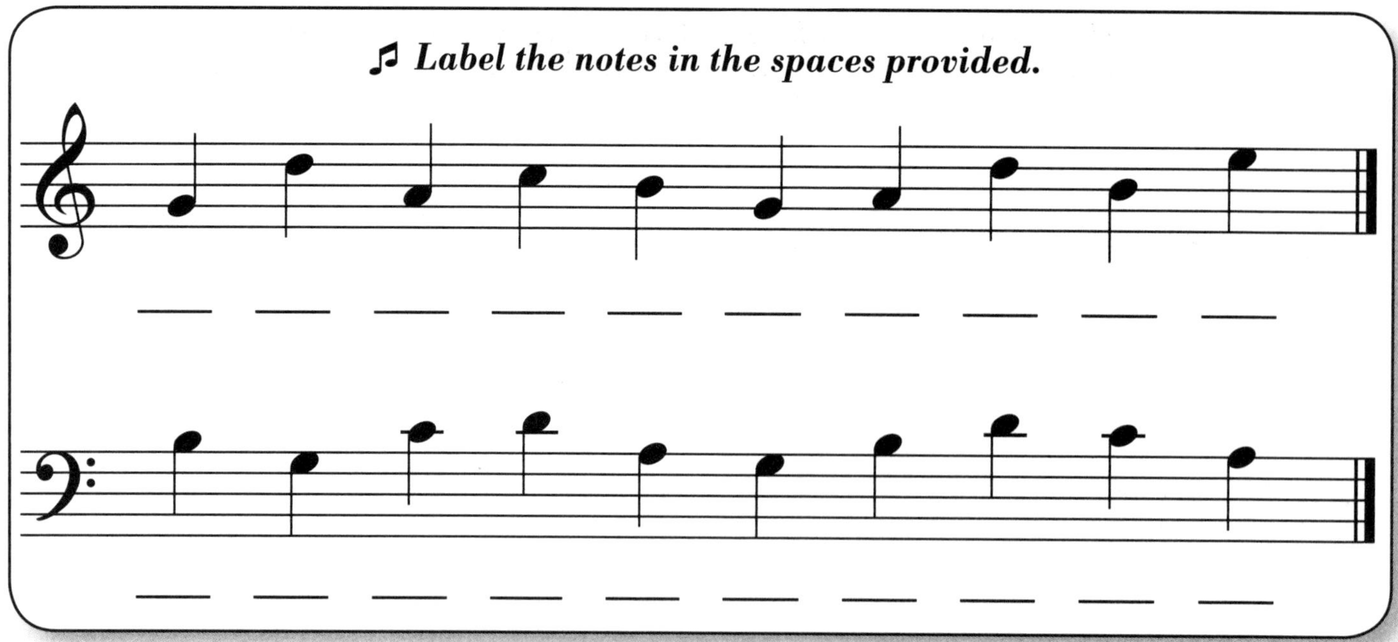

16b. Lead the Way!

♫ ***Follow the directions to complete the piece below.***

1. Add stems to all of the notes and trace the slurs.
2. Play the melody and add chord symbols.
3. Play again and improvise the left hand using the chord symbols.

16c. Power Play

♫ ***Play the examples below. Use the fingerings provided.***

EXAMPLE 1:

EXAMPLE 2:

EXAMPLE 3:

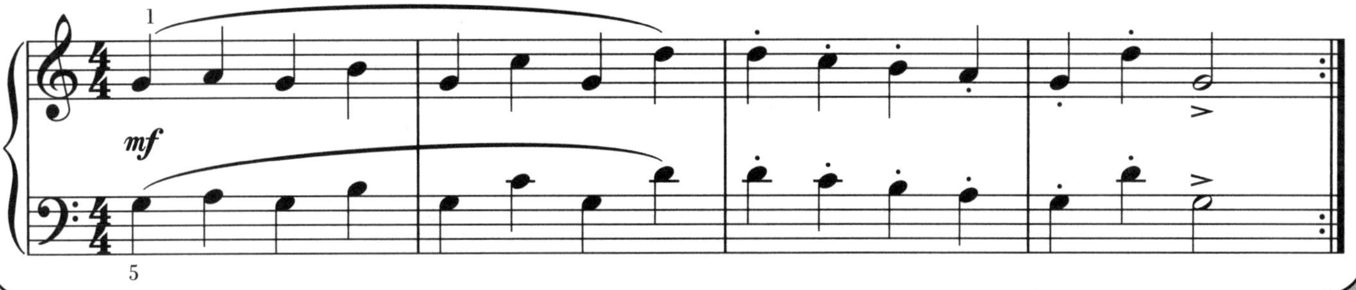

16d. Composition Corner

♫ ***Compose measures 5–7. Add chord symbols and play the piece.***

17a. Ready to Review

♫ ***Label each interval as a m3, M3, P4, or P5.***

17b. Transposition

In *Alouette*, you played the same melody in two different positions: C position and G position. **Transposition** is the process of moving a collection of notes (a melody) up or down in pitch while keeping the same intervals between the notes. Study the example below.

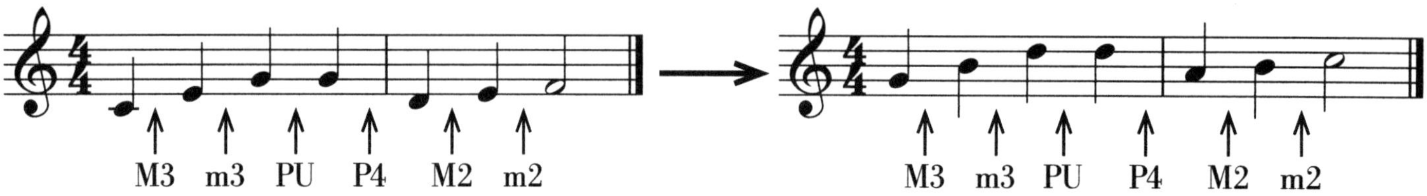

M3 m3 PU P4 M2 m2 → M3 m3 PU P4 M2 m2

♫ ***Transpose each melody and notate it on the empty staff. The starting note is given.***

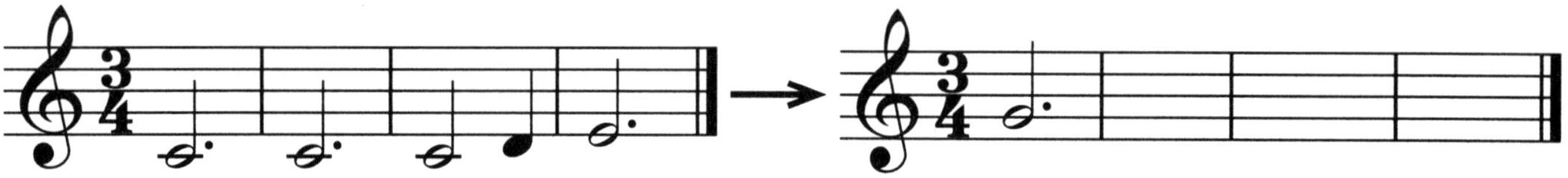

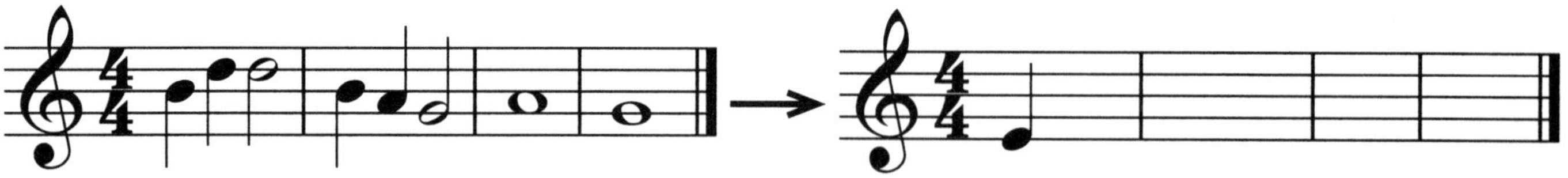

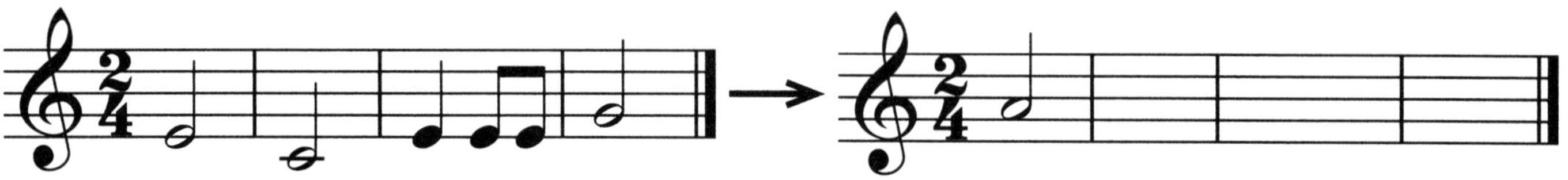

17c. Power Play

♫ *Play the examples below. Use the fingerings provided.*

EXAMPLE 1:

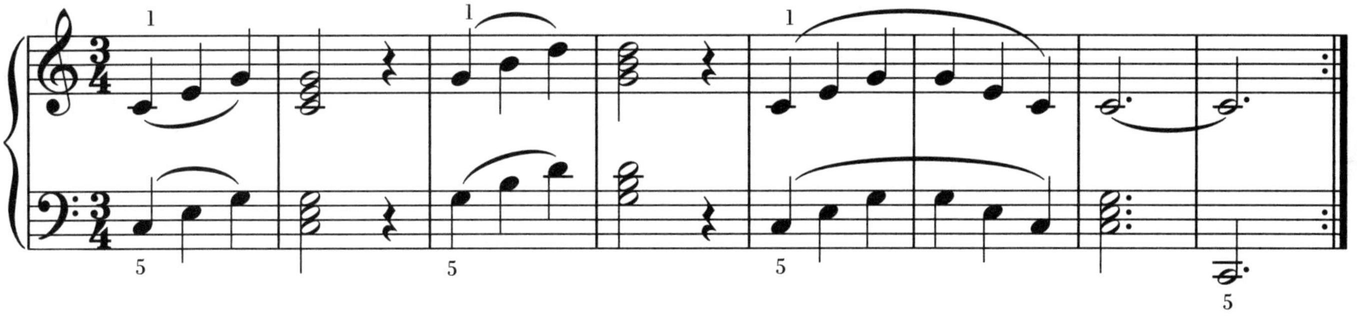

EXAMPLE 2:

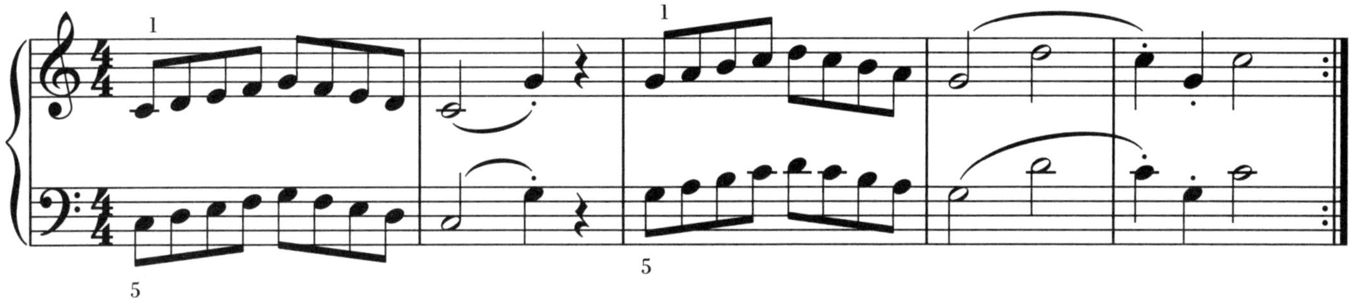

17d. Composition Corner

♫ *Transpose the melody below to G position. Add chord symbols and play the piece.**

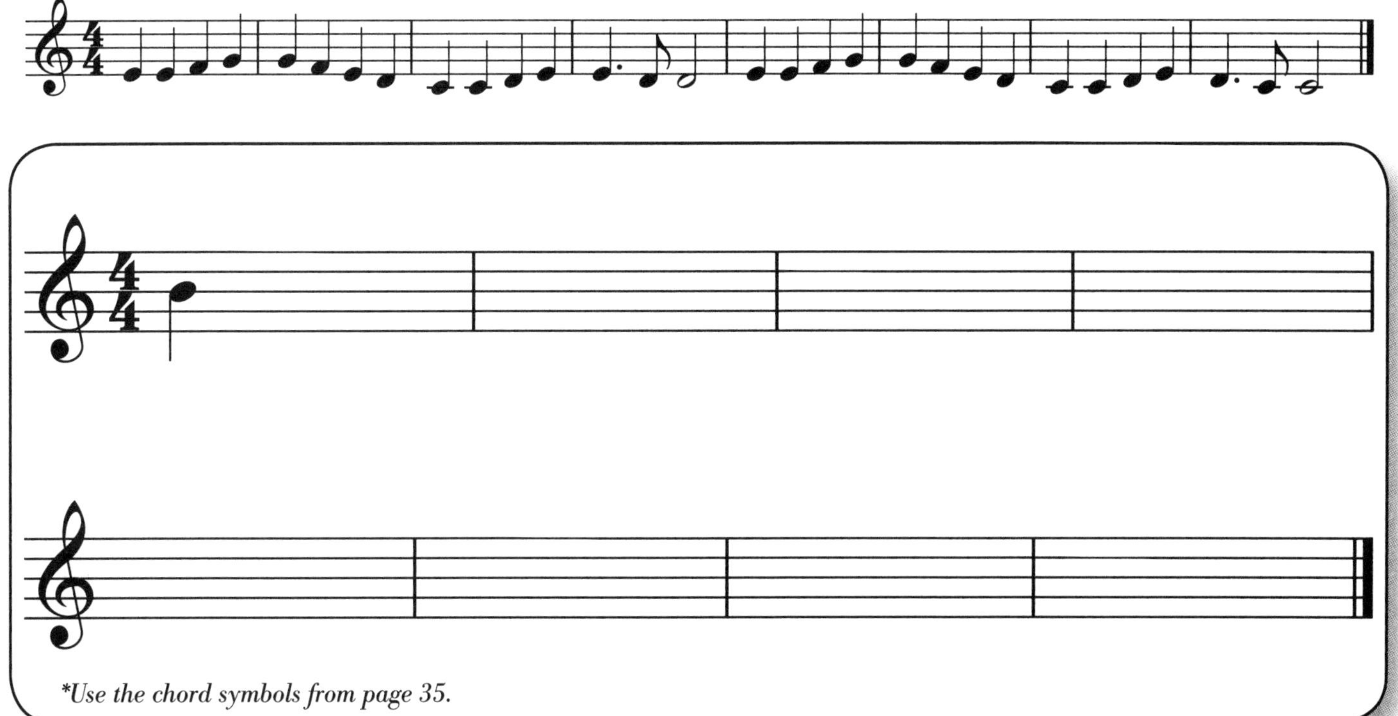

**Use the chord symbols from page 35.*

18a. Ready to Review

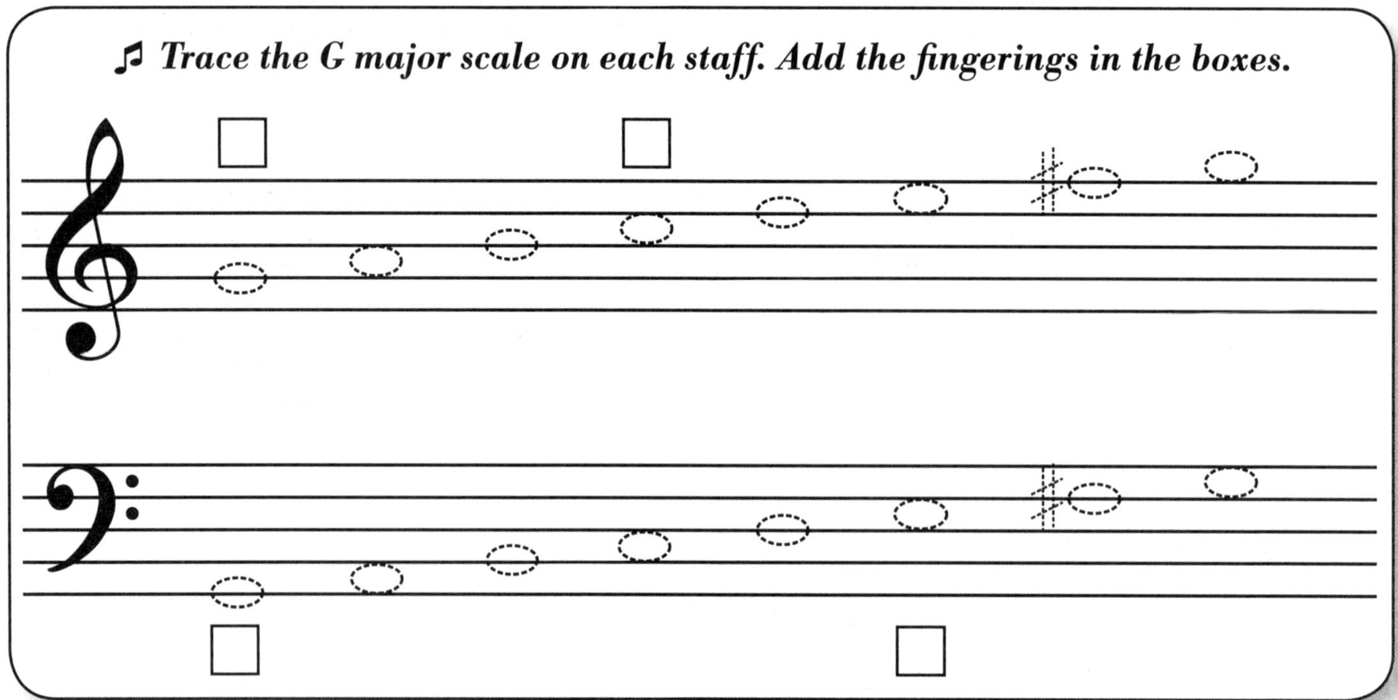
♫ *Trace the G major scale on each staff. Add the fingerings in the boxes.*

18b. Lead the Way!

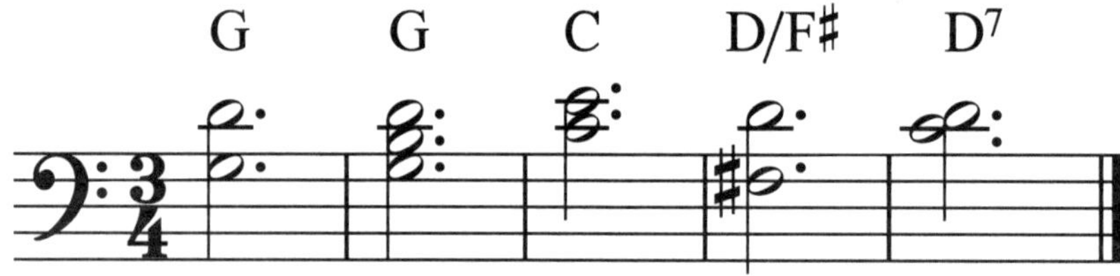

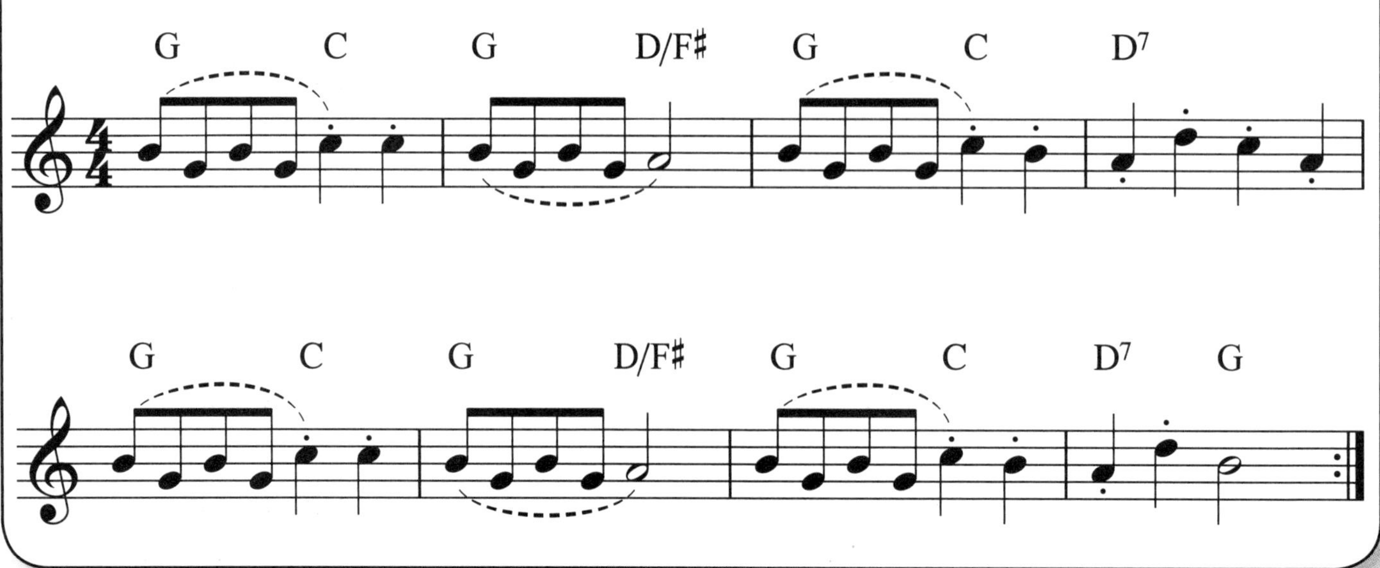
♫ *Trace the slurs. Play the melody and improvise the left hand using the chord symbols and the options above.*

18c. Power Play

♫ ***Let's practice playing the G major scale in contrary motion with both hands.****

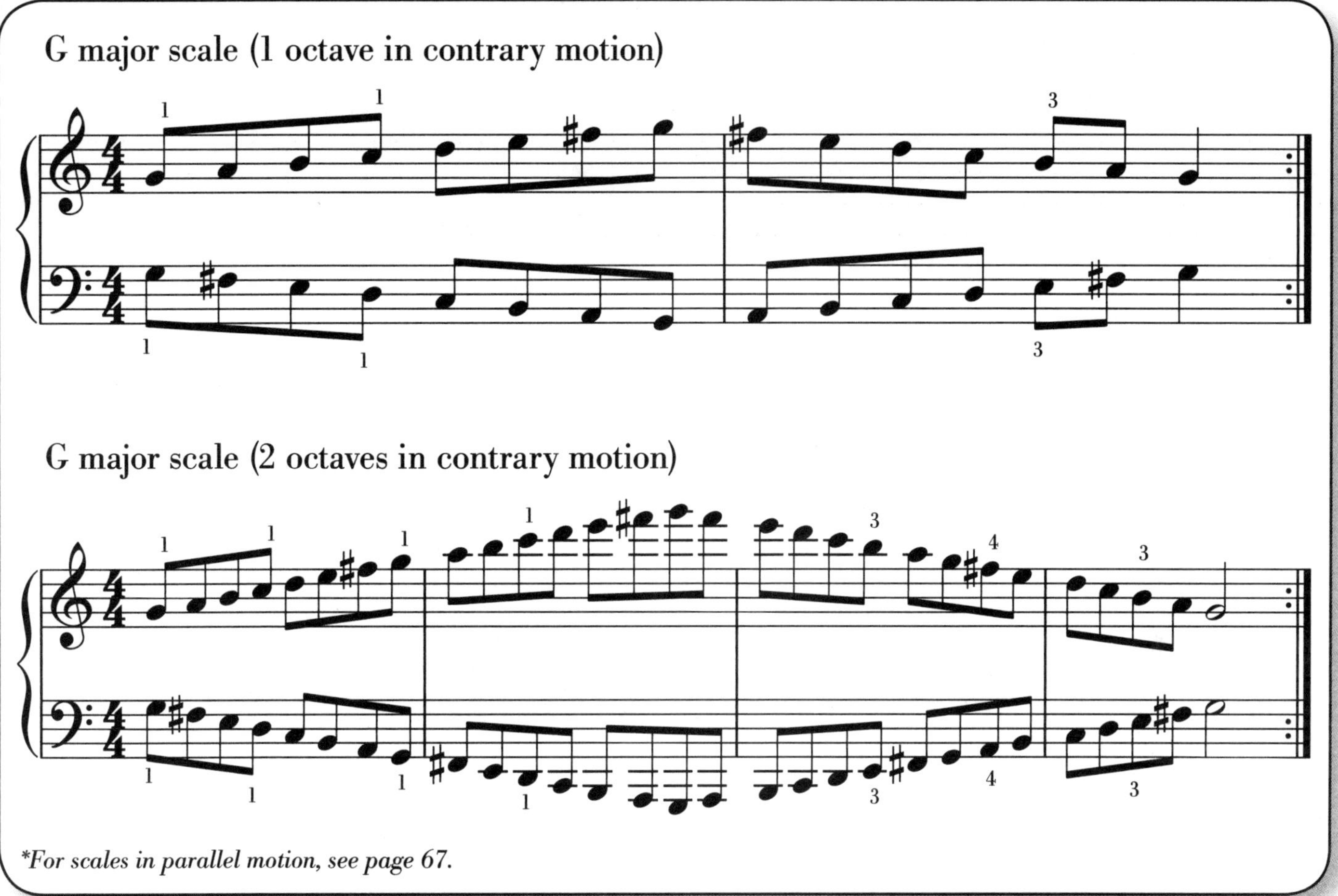

**For scales in parallel motion, see page 67.*

18d. I'm All Ears!

Major = bright, cheerful sounds **Minor** = dark, melancholy sounds

♫ ***Your teacher will play a major or minor triad. Circle what you hear.***

1. I hear a: **major triad** ***or*** **minor triad**

2. I hear a: **major triad** ***or*** **minor triad**

3. I hear a: **major triad** ***or*** **minor triad**

4. I hear a: **major triad** ***or*** **minor triad**

5. I hear a: **major triad** ***or*** **minor triad**

19a. Ready to Review

♫ ***Draw the G major key signature on each grand staff. Follow the example.***

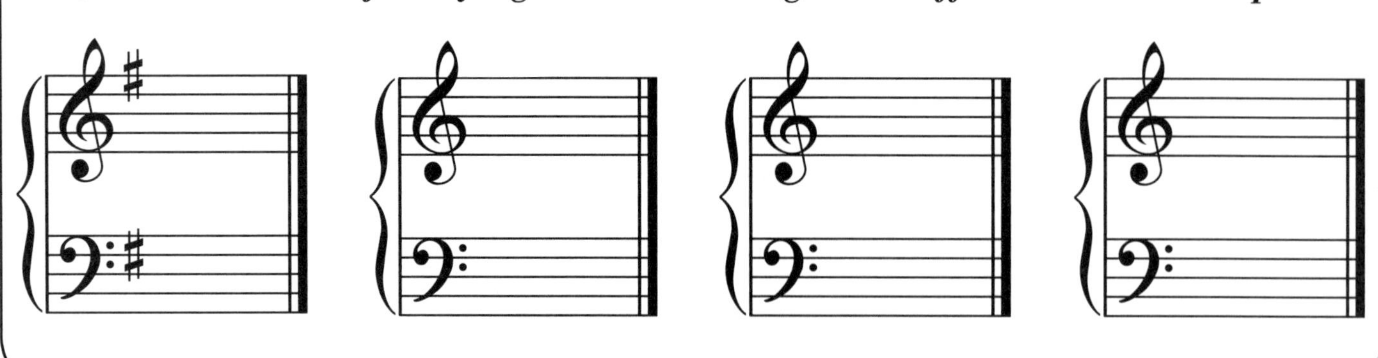

19b. Lead the Way!

As we learned earlier in this book, each time signature has natural accenting patterns. In 3/4 time, the first beat is strong, and the second and third beats are weak (unaccented).

♫ ***Harmonize the melody using the chord symbols. In empty measures, notate the chord as a dotted half note. In measures that start with a rest, place two quarter notes on the weak beats. Play the piece.***

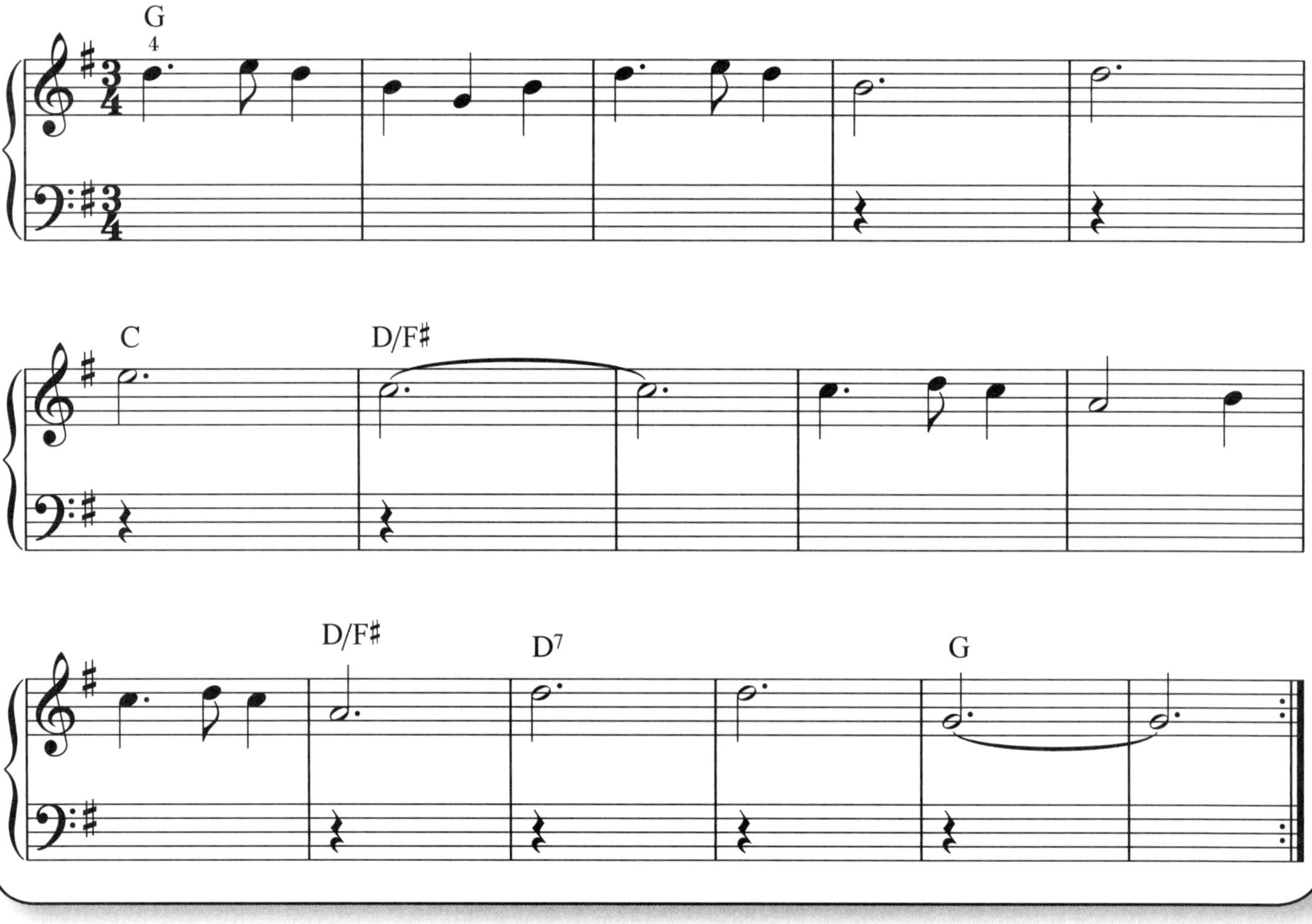

19c. Power Play

♫ ***Play the examples below. Use the fingerings and chord symbols provided.***

19d. Composition Corner

♫ ***Transpose the melody below to the key of C major. Add slurs, staccatos, fingerings, and chord symbols. Play the piece.***

Triads: Root Position

When a **triad** is stacked in thirds it is called a **root position triad.** On the staff: line-line-line or space-space-space. Root position triads have three parts:

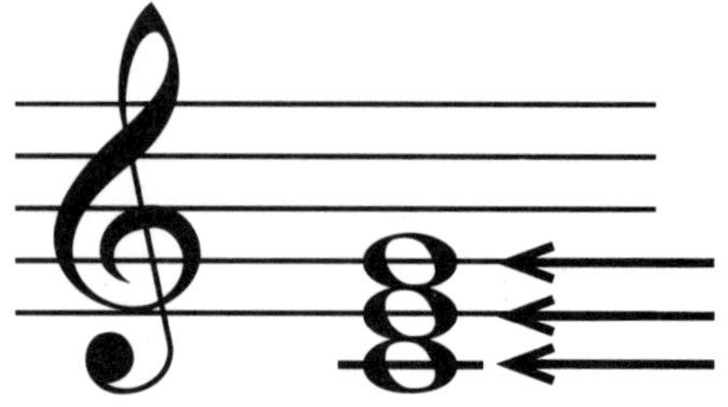

Fifth = the top note; a 5th above the root.
Third = the middle note; a 3rd above the root.
Root = the note on which the triad is built.

♫ ***Build triads above each given note. Color the triad root your favorite color.***

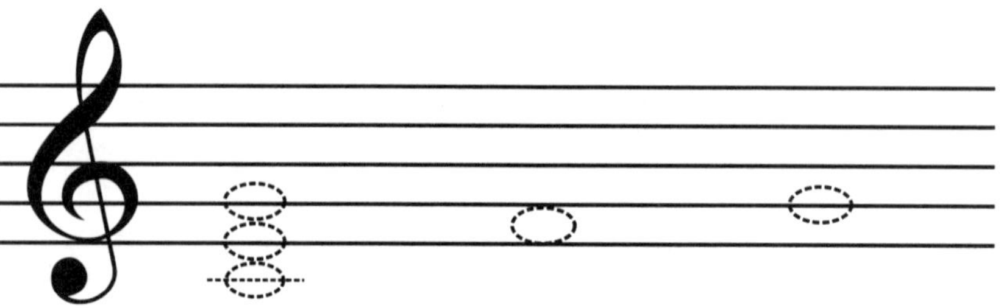

Triads: First Inversion

A triad can be in root position or an **inversion**. In an inversion, the lowest note is not the root. In a **first inversion triad,** the third is the lowest note and the root is shifted up an octave to the top of the triad.

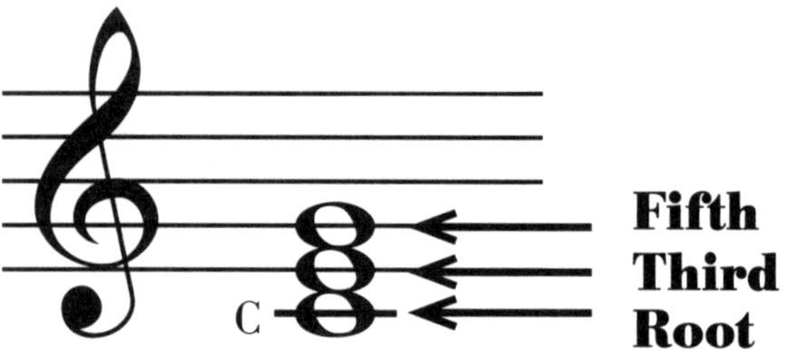

Root position

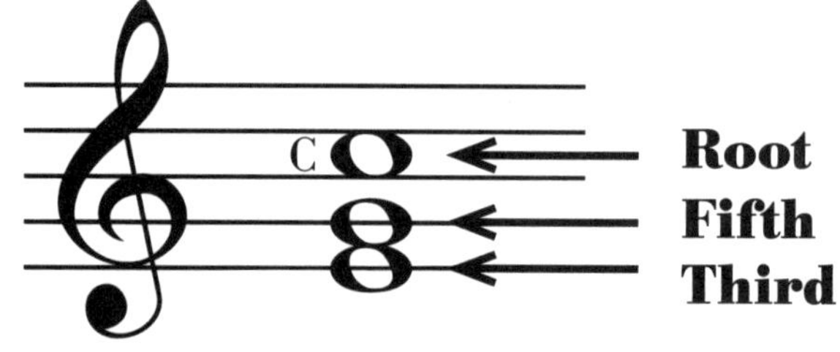

First (1st) inversion

♫ ***Change the root position triads to first inversion. Color all the triad roots.***

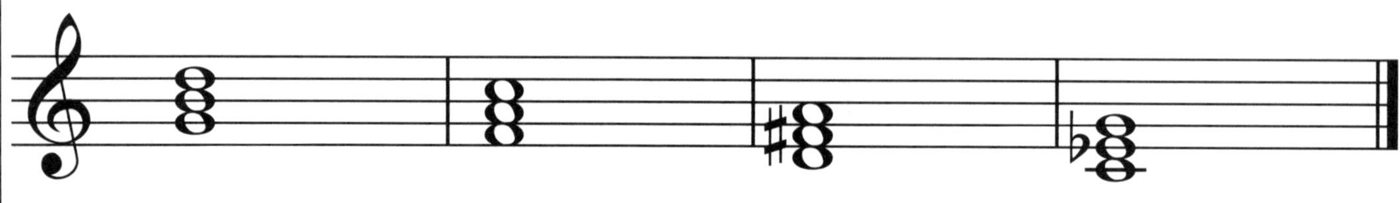

Root 1st inv. Root 1st inv. Root 1st inv. Root 1st inv.

Triads: Second Inversion

In a **second inversion triad,** the fifth is the lowest note. To change a first inversion triad to second inversion, the third is shifted up an octave to the top of the triad.

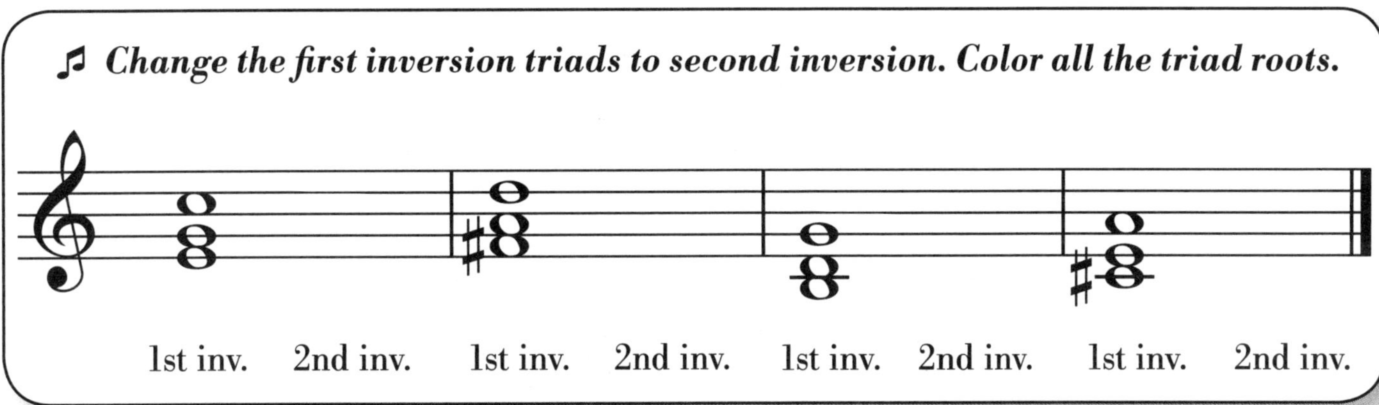

Identifying Inversions

Inversions of triads have specific intervals between each note. Knowing these patterns will help you quickly identify the inversion.

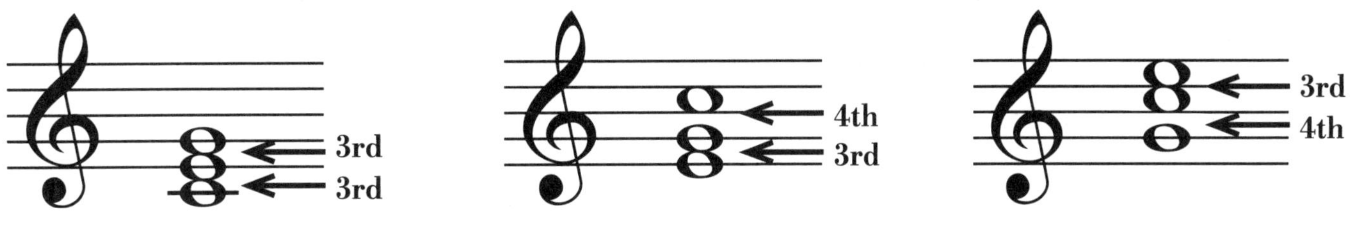

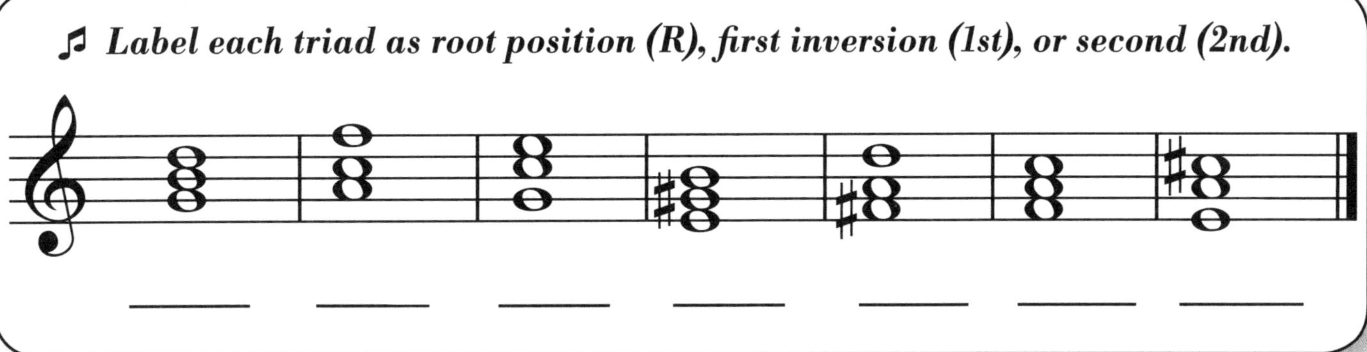

20a. Ready to Review

♫ *Circle the root position triads. Color the triad roots.*

♫ *Complete the first inversion triads. Color the triad roots.*

♫ *Complete the second inversion triads. Color the triad roots.*

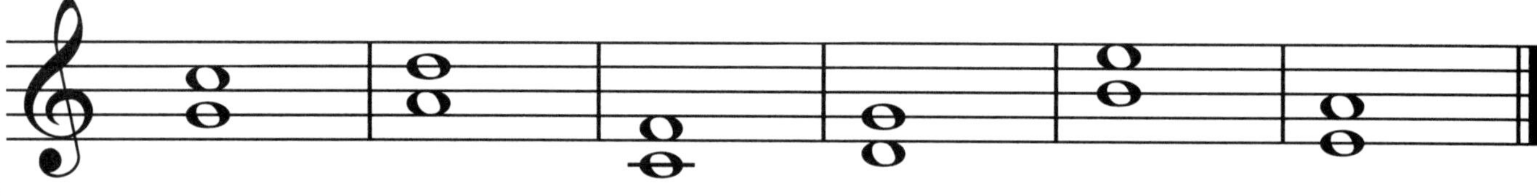

20b. Minor & Major 6ths

Minor 6th (m6)
On the piano = 8 half steps

Major 6th (M6)
On the piano = 9 half steps

♫ *Label each interval as a minor sixth (m6) or a major sixth (M6).*

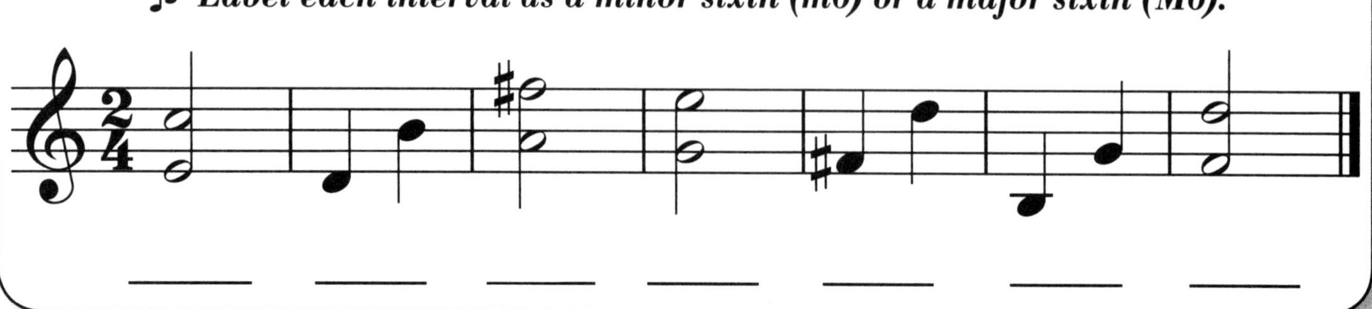

______ ______ ______ ______ ______ ______ ______

20c. Power Play

Play the examples below. Use the fingerings provided.

EXAMPLE 1:

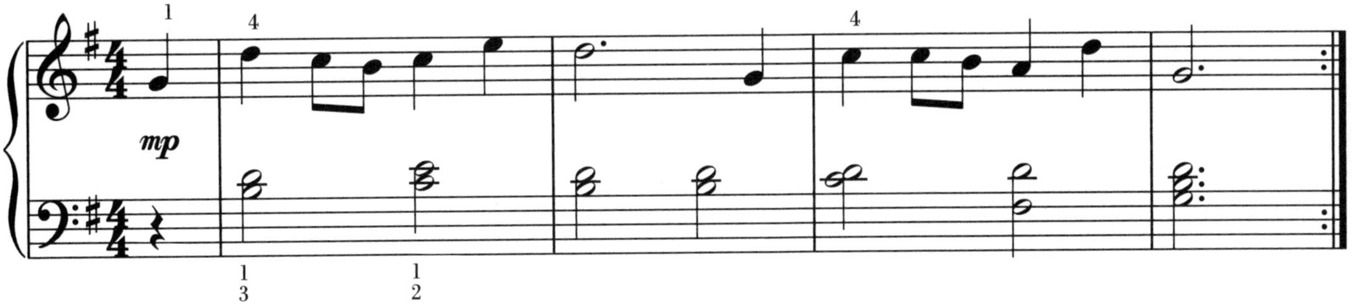

mp

EXAMPLE 2:

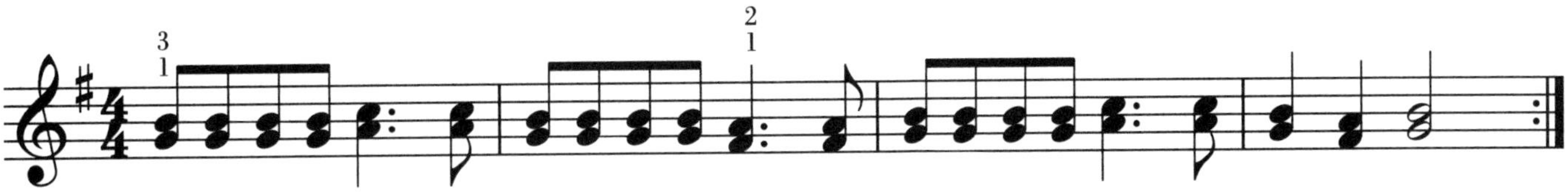

EXAMPLE 3:

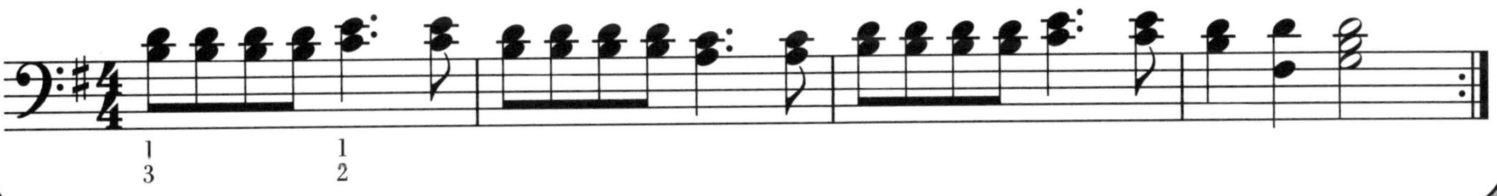

20d. I'm All Ears!

Your teacher will play each example, adding the second note of each melodic interval above or below the given note. Complete the measure to notate what you hear.*

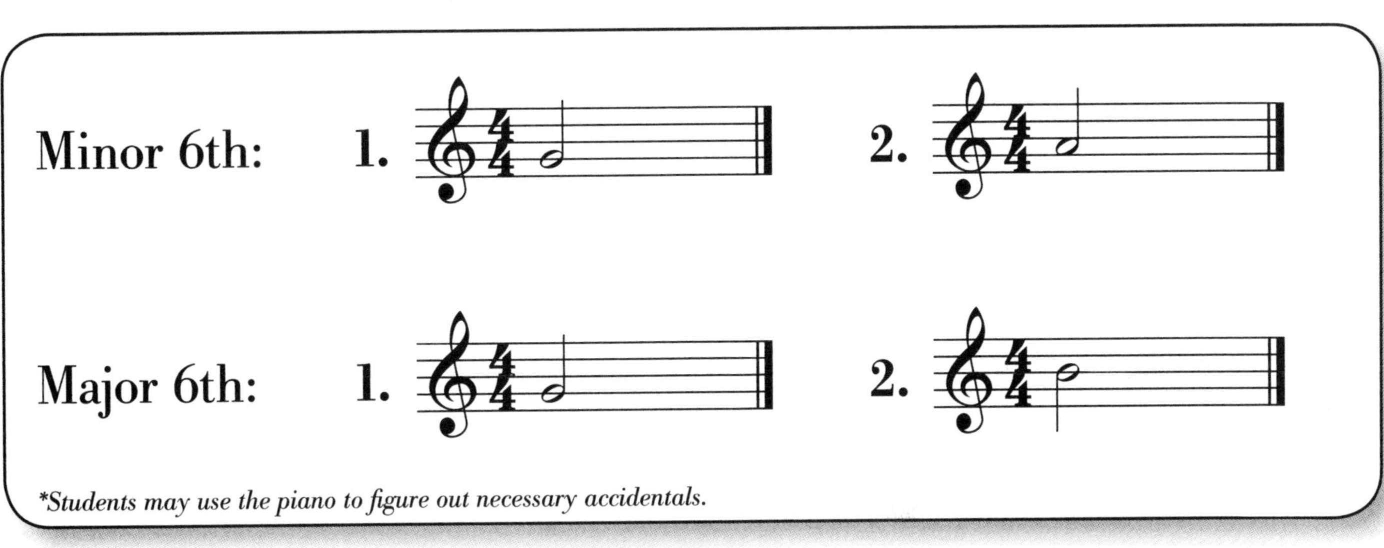

**Students may use the piano to figure out necessary accidentals.*

Major & Minor Triads

We have already worked on hearing the difference between major and minor triads. Now let's learn how they are built! Major and minor triads each have a unique pattern of intervals between the notes. When you name a triad, the letter name is always the triad root.

C major triad **C minor triad**

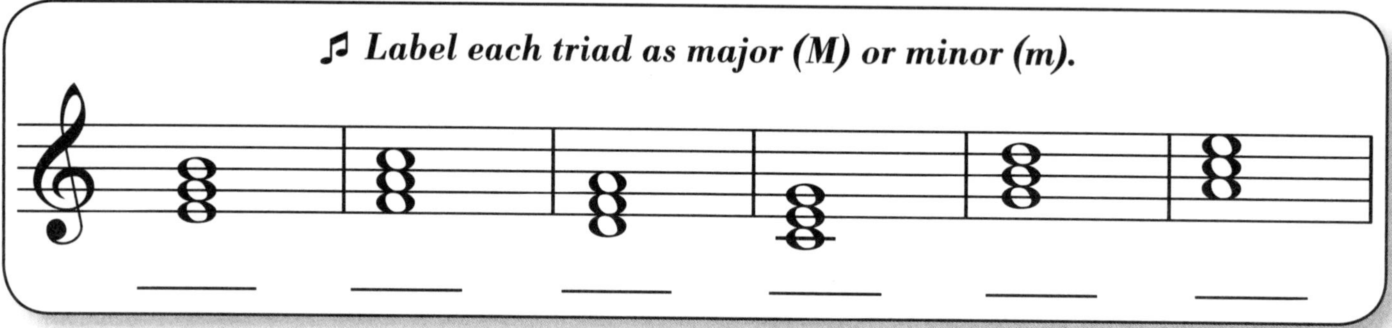

Music Analysis: Traditional

Each step of a major scale is called a **scale degree**. We use numbers to label each scale degree. Triads can be built on each scale degree; in traditional music analysis these triads are labeled with **roman numerals** placed underneath the staff to show the function of the chord within the key. Large roman numerals mean the triad built on that scale degree is major. Small roman numerals mean the triad is minor.

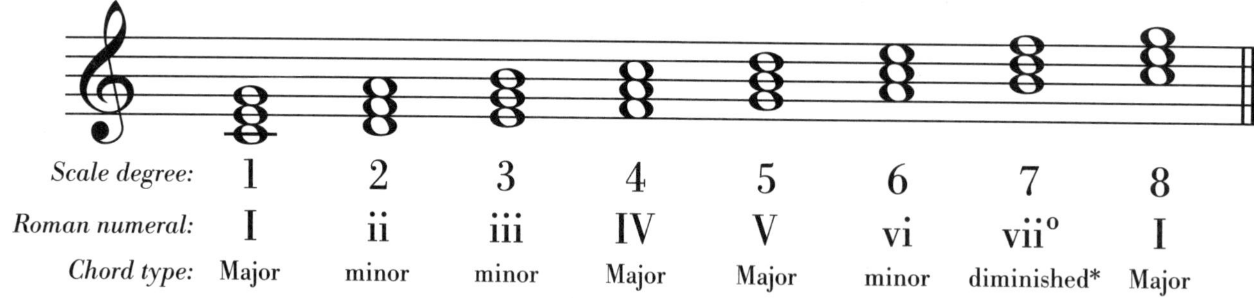

Scale degree:	1	2	3	4	5	6	7	8
Roman numeral:	I	ii	iii	IV	V	vi	vii°	I
Chord type:	Major	minor	minor	Major	Major	minor	diminished*	Major

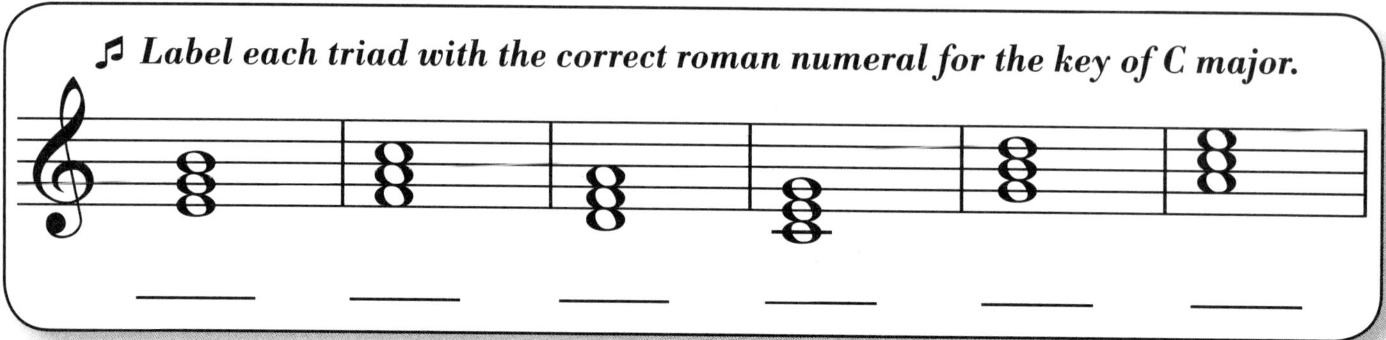

**This will be explained later.*

Music Analysis: Pop & Jazz

When analyzing or writing a lead sheet for a piece of pop or jazz music, we use chord symbols above the staff to label the chords and indicate what left-hand notes should be played. Major chords are labeled with just the letter name of the chord root. Minor chords are labeled with the chord root followed by a small "m." Diminished chords are labeled with the chord root followed by "dim." or a degree sign (°). We will learn about diminished chords later.

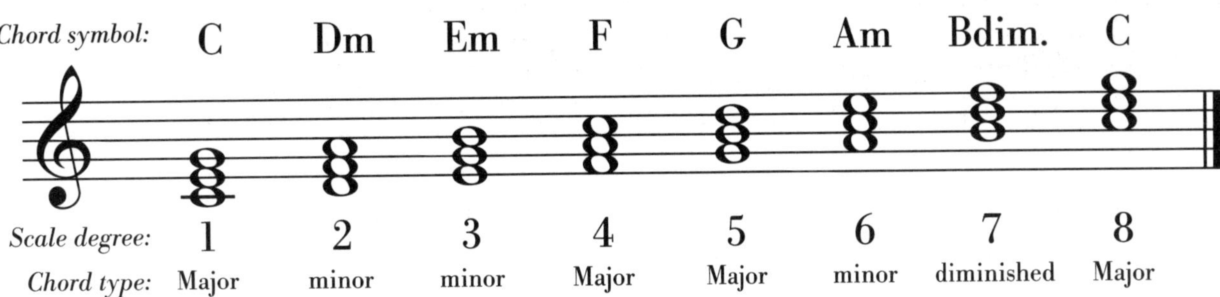

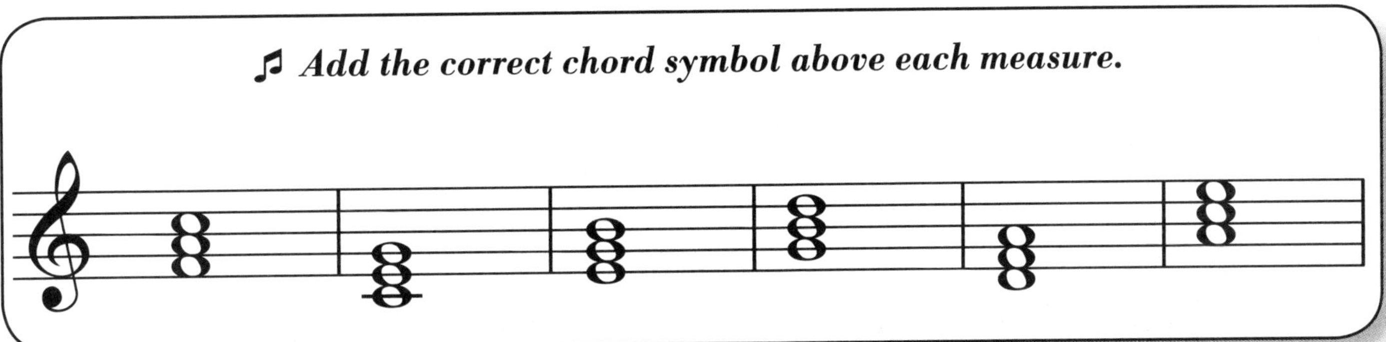

Music Analysis: Inversions

Inversions of triads and chords are labeled differently for traditional* and pop or jazz analysis.

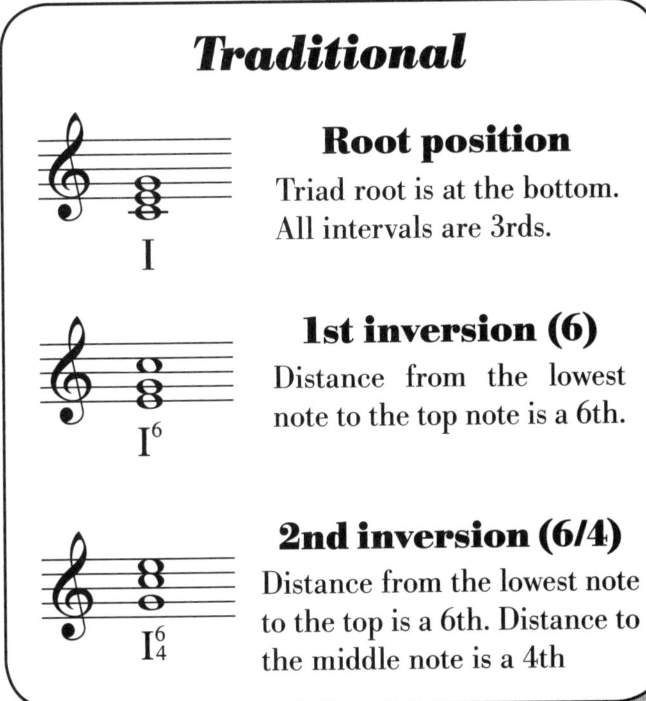

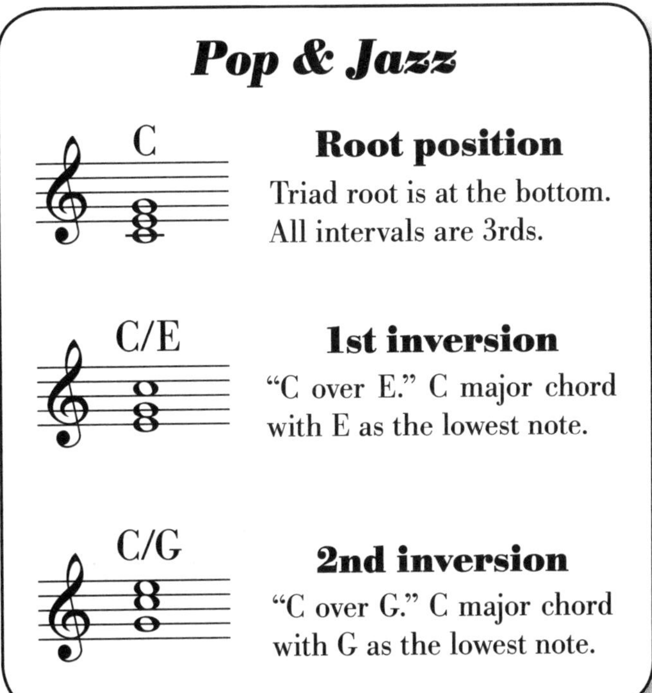

*This system is called figured bass notation.

21a. Primary Chords

Primary chords are considered the strongest chords of a key. In major keys, these chords are always major and are built on the scale degrees 1, 4, and 5. The chord built on scale degree 1 is called the **tonic**. The chord built on scale degree 4 is called the **subdominant**. The chord built on scale degree 5 is called the **dominant**.

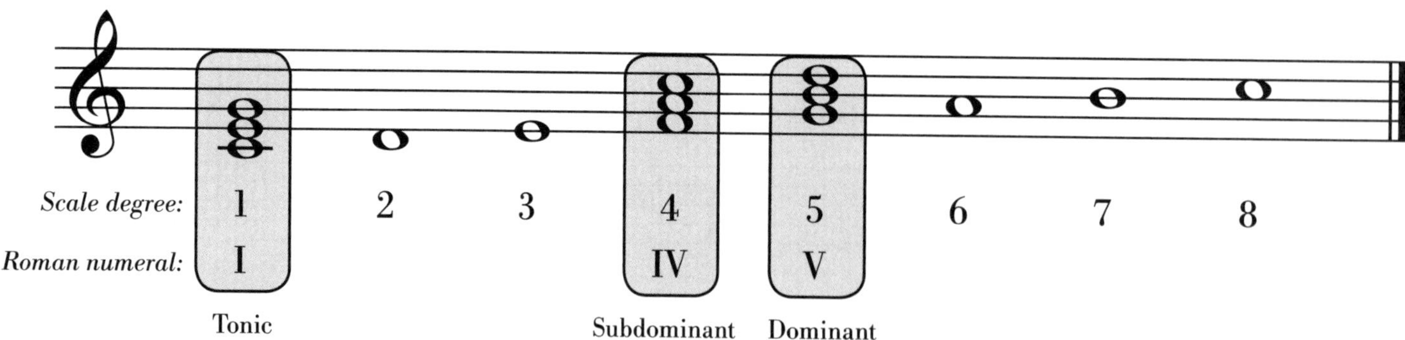

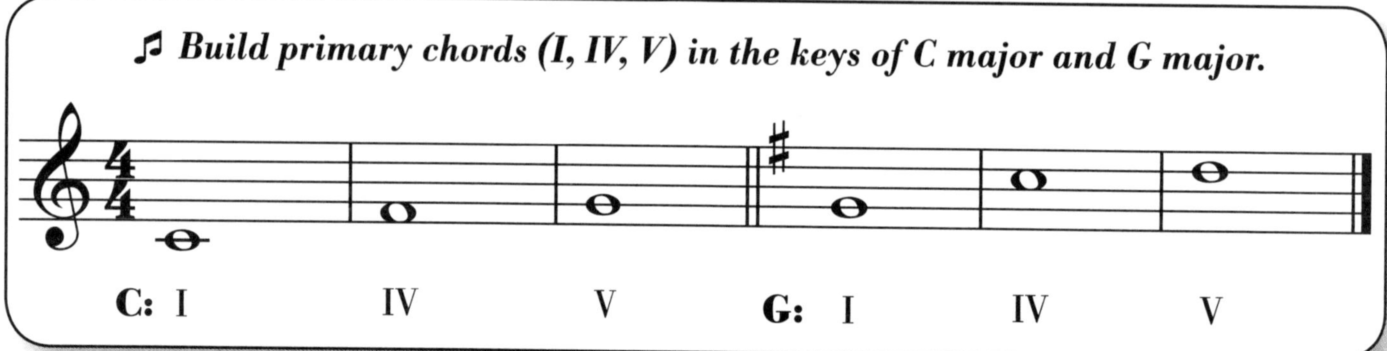

21b. Chord Progressions: C Major

A **chord progression** is a sequence of chords. You will learn to play two chord progressions using primary chords in the key of C major: one with the dominant chord (V), and one with the **dominant seventh** (V7), which you will learn more about in the next book. Primary chord progressions use inversions to encourage smooth **voice leading**; this is more efficient than using only root position triads.

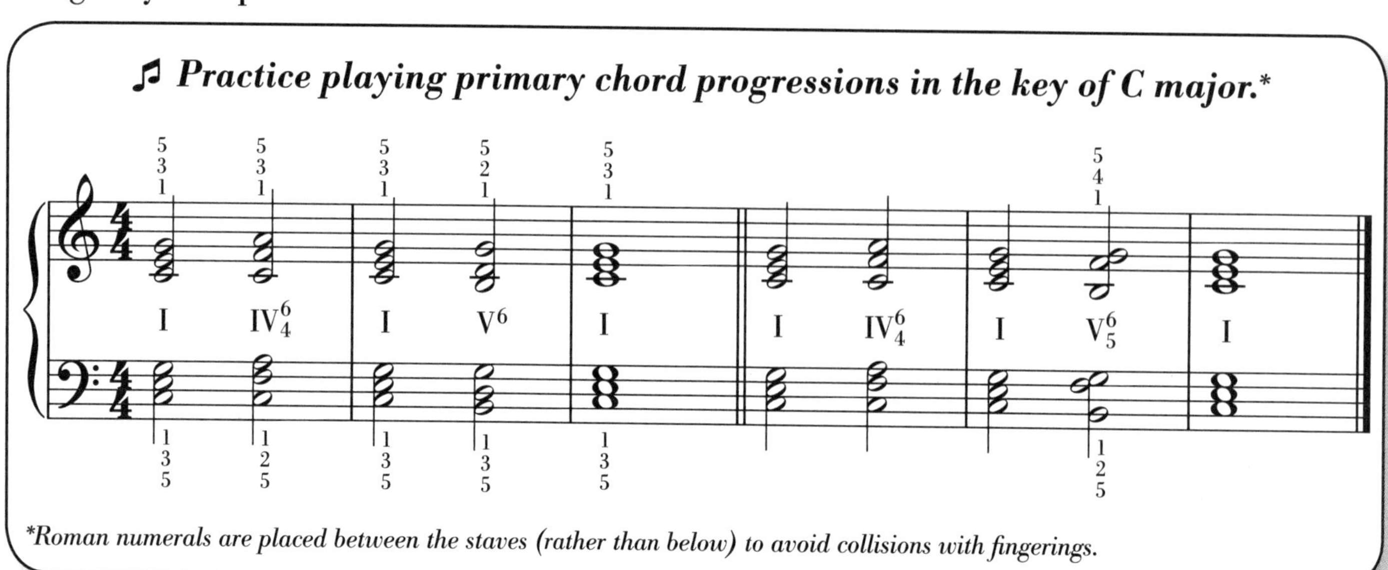

*Roman numerals are placed between the staves (rather than below) to avoid collisions with fingerings.

21c. Chord Progressions: G Major

♫ ***Practice playing primary chord progressions in the key of G major. Reminder: the F-sharp will not be marked since it is part of the key signature.***

I
IV$^6_4$
I
V^6
I
I
IV$^6_4$
I
V$^6_5$
I

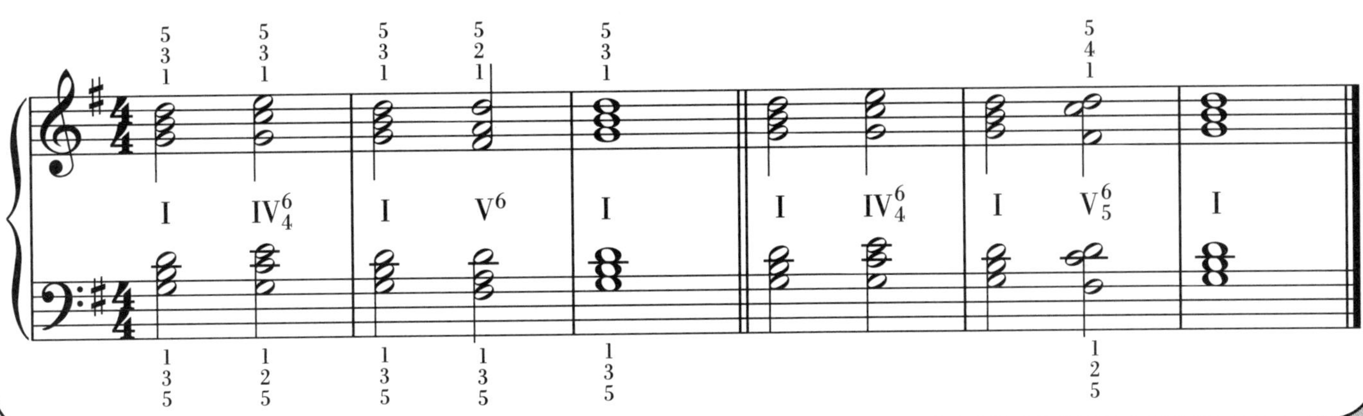

21d. Composition Corner

♫ ***Transpose the given melody to the key of G major on the staff below. Add the missing chord symbols, transposed to the new key, above the staff.***

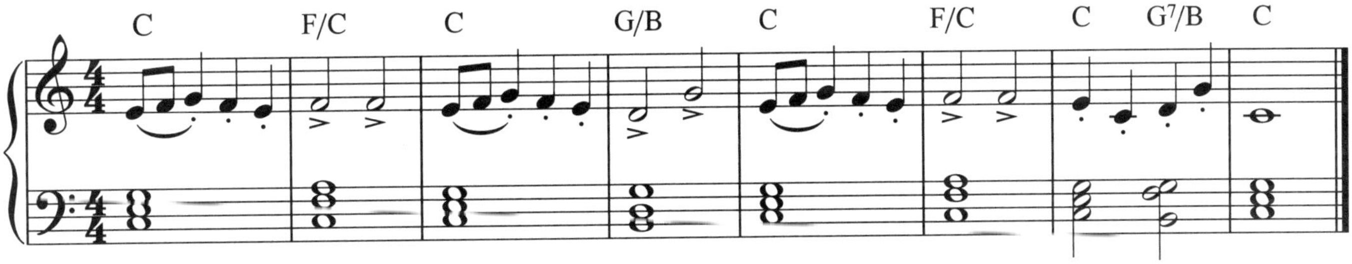

C
F/C
C
G/B
C
F/C
C
G^7/B
C

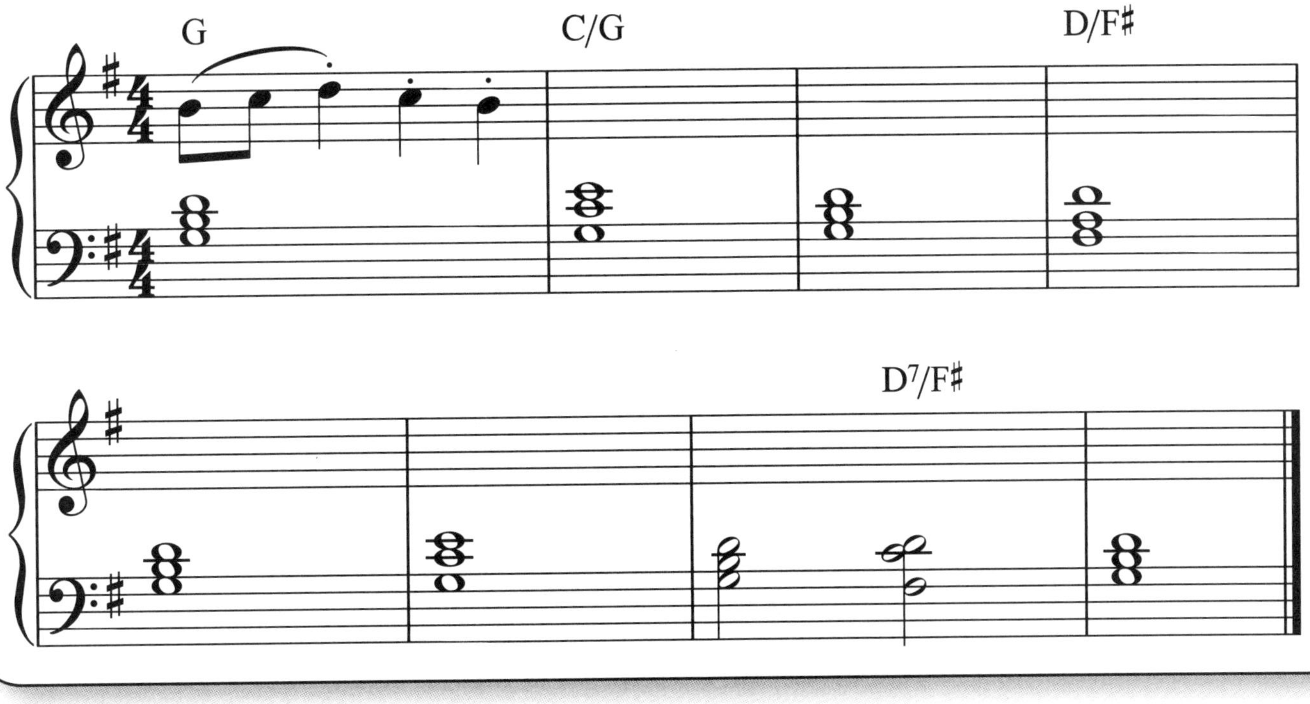

G
C/G
D/F♯
D^7/F♯

22a. Ready to Review

♫ *Label the notes in the spaces provided.*

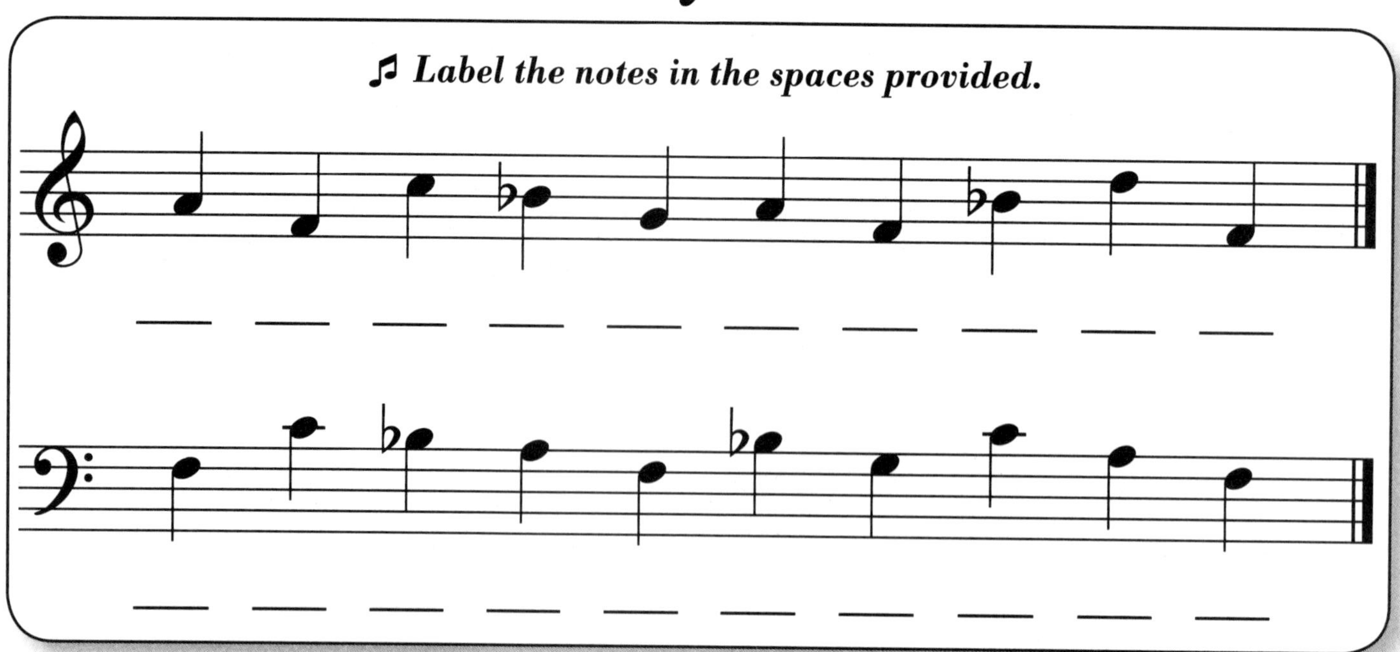

22b. Lead the Way!

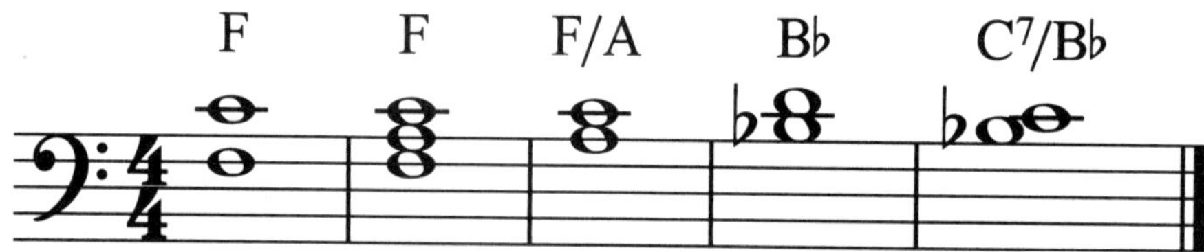

♫ *Follow the directions to complete the piece below.*

1. Trace the slurs.
2. Play the melody and then add chord symbols.
3. Play again and improvise the left hand using the chord symbols.

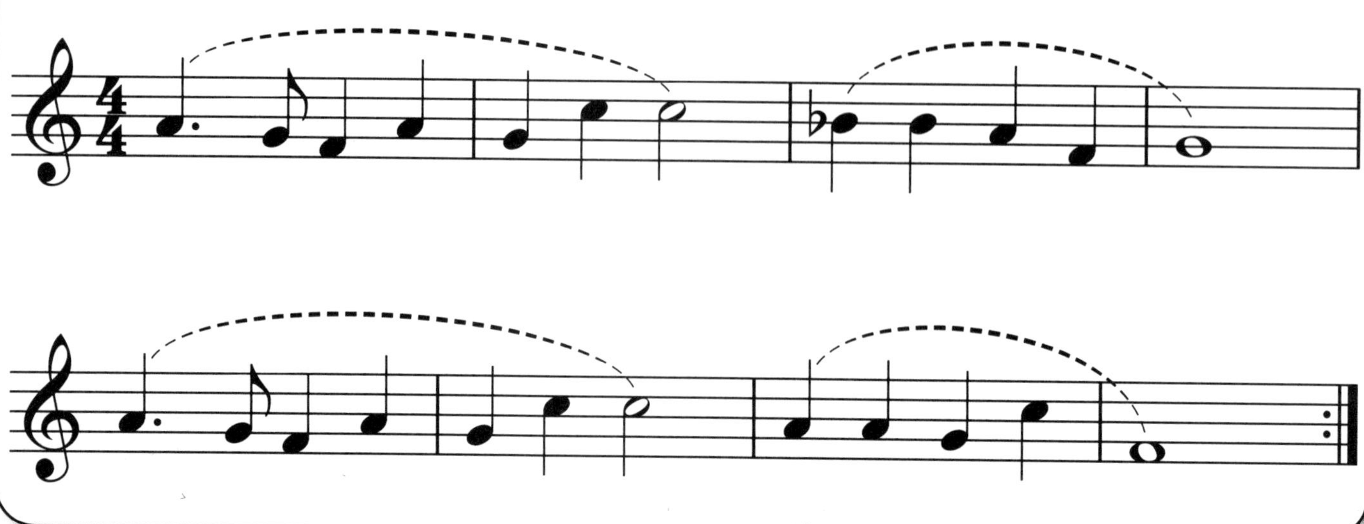

22c. Power Play

♫ ***Play the examples below. Use the fingerings provided.***

EXAMPLE 1:

EXAMPLE 2:

EXAMPLE 3:

22d. Composition Corner

♫ ***Transpose the melody below to F position. Add chord symbols, using the options from page 51, and play the piece.***

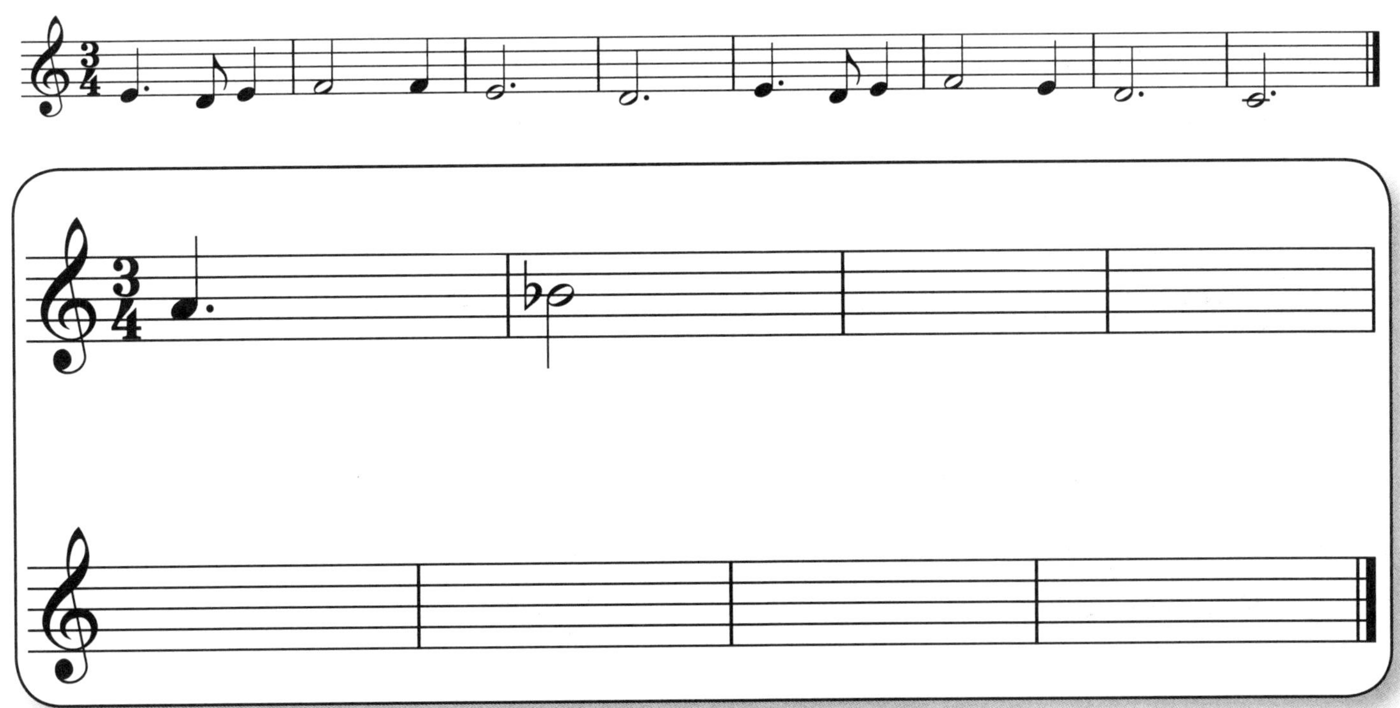

Review: Major & Minor Triads

C major triad

C minor triad

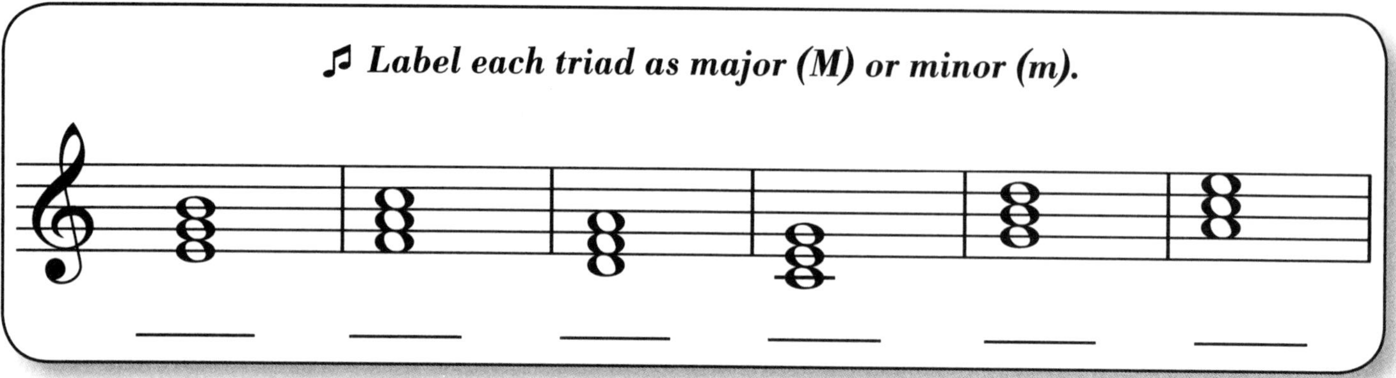

Building Major & Minor Triads

1. Draw root position triad using the given root name.
2. Use the piano to count the half steps between each note of the triad.
3. If necessary, add an accidental to the triad third to form a major or minor triad.

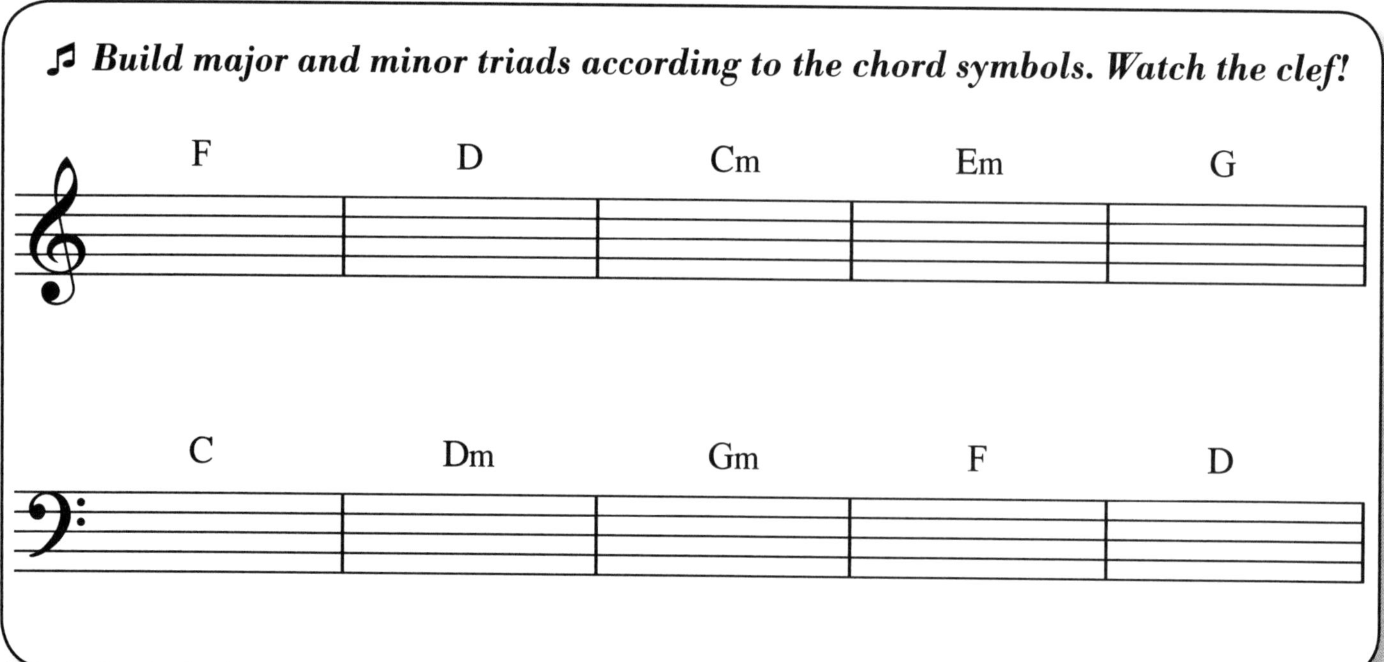

Review: Inversions (Traditional)

Root position

1st inversion (6)

2nd inversion (6/4)

♫ *Notate the first and second inversions of the given root position triads.**

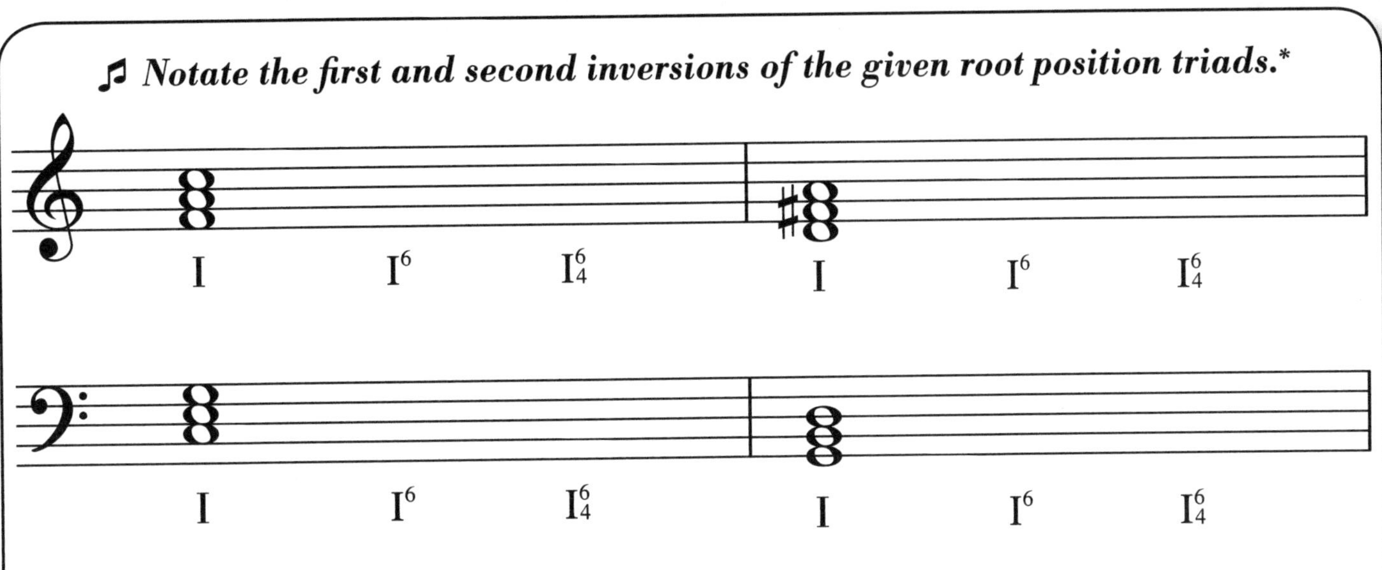

**Inversions can be shifted 8vb to avoid ledger lines.*

Review: Inversions (Chord Symbols)

Root position

1st inversion

2nd inversion

♫ *Add the correct chord symbol above the inversion after each root position triad.*

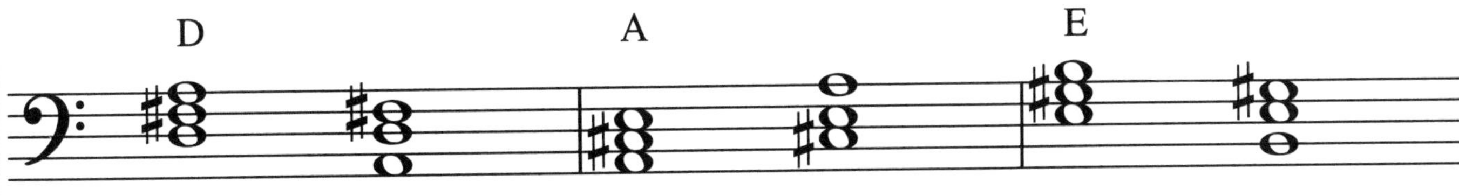

23a. Ready to Review

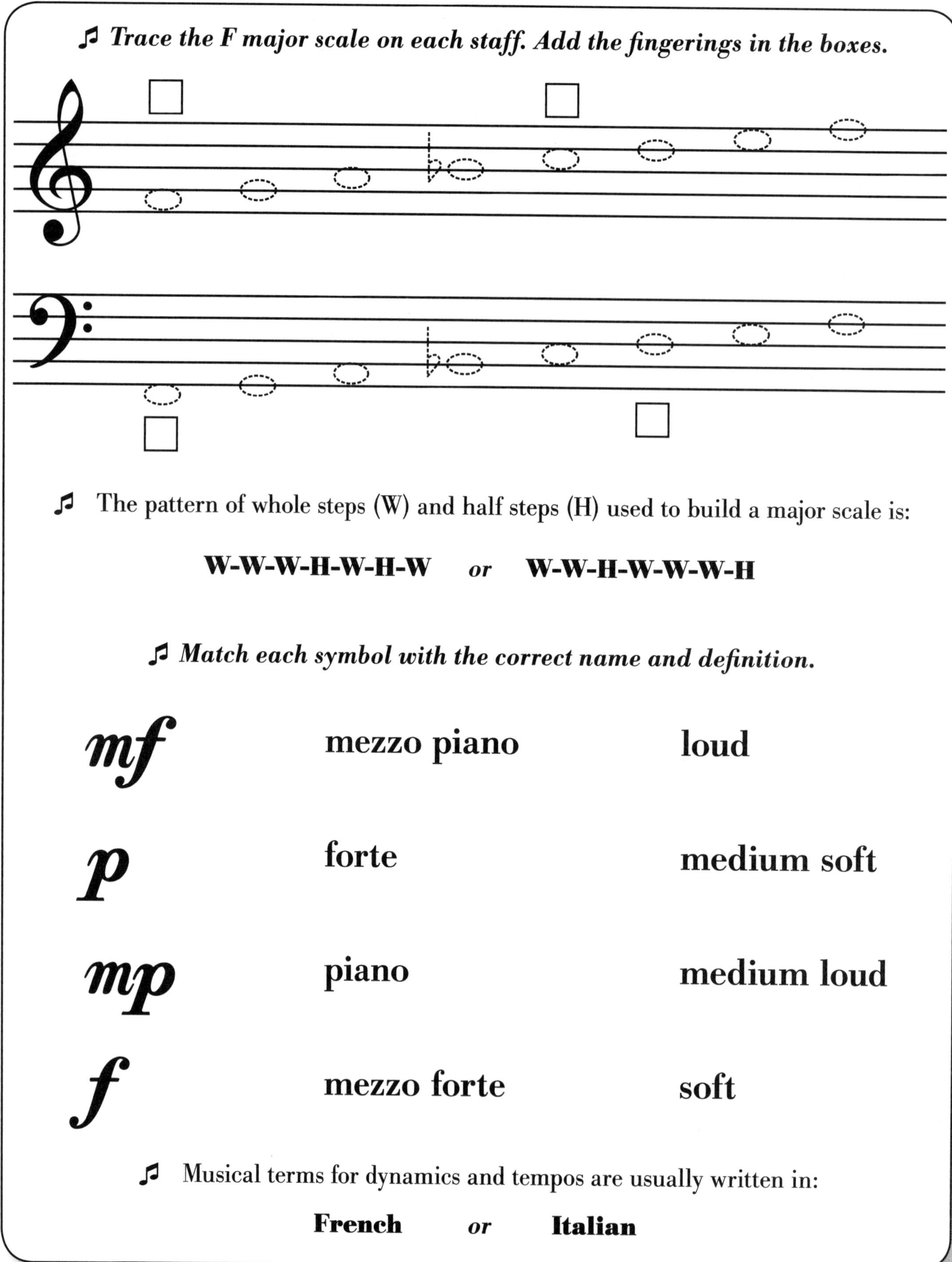

23b. Power Play

♫ ***Let's practice playing the F major scale hands separately in two octaves.****

23c. I'm All Ears!

Major = bright, cheerful sounds   **Minor** = dark, melancholy sounds

♫ ***Your teacher will play a major or minor triad. Circle what you hear.***

1. I hear a: major triad *or* minor triad

2. I hear a: major triad *or* minor triad

3. I hear a: major triad *or* minor triad

4. I hear a: major triad *or* minor triad

5. I hear a: major triad *or* minor triad

24a. Ready to Review

♫ ***Draw the F major key signature on each grand staff. Follow the example.***

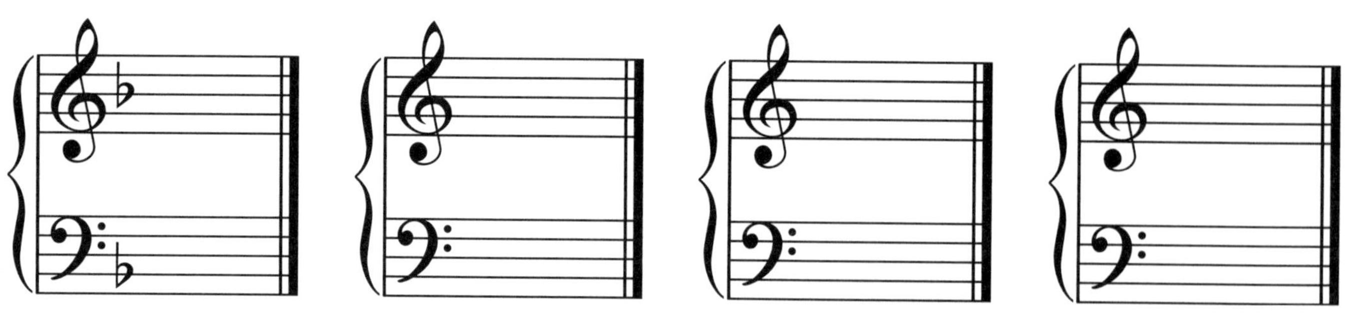

24b. Analyze This

♫ ***Follow the directions to analyze the piece below.***

1. How many slurs can you find? ______ How many staccatos? ______

2. What key is the piece in? Add the letter name under the key signature in the blank.

3. Analyze the chords by adding roman numerals, including inversions, in the spaces provided. The first and last chords are completed for you. *Note: It is common to omit the fifth of a chord and only play the root and the third.*

24c. Power Play

Play the examples below. Use the fingerings provided.

EXAMPLE 1:

mf

EXAMPLE 2:

mp

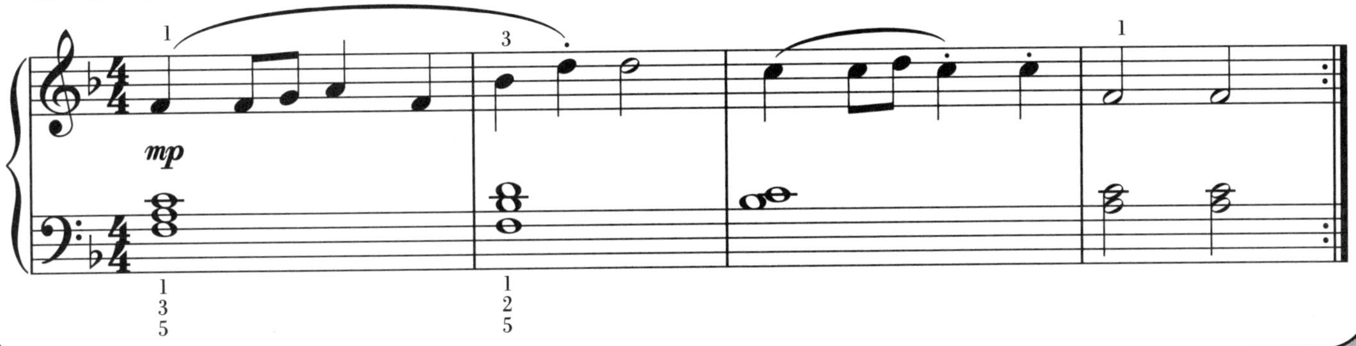

24d. Composition Corner

Compose a melody over the given chords. Add dynamics and articulations. Play the piece.

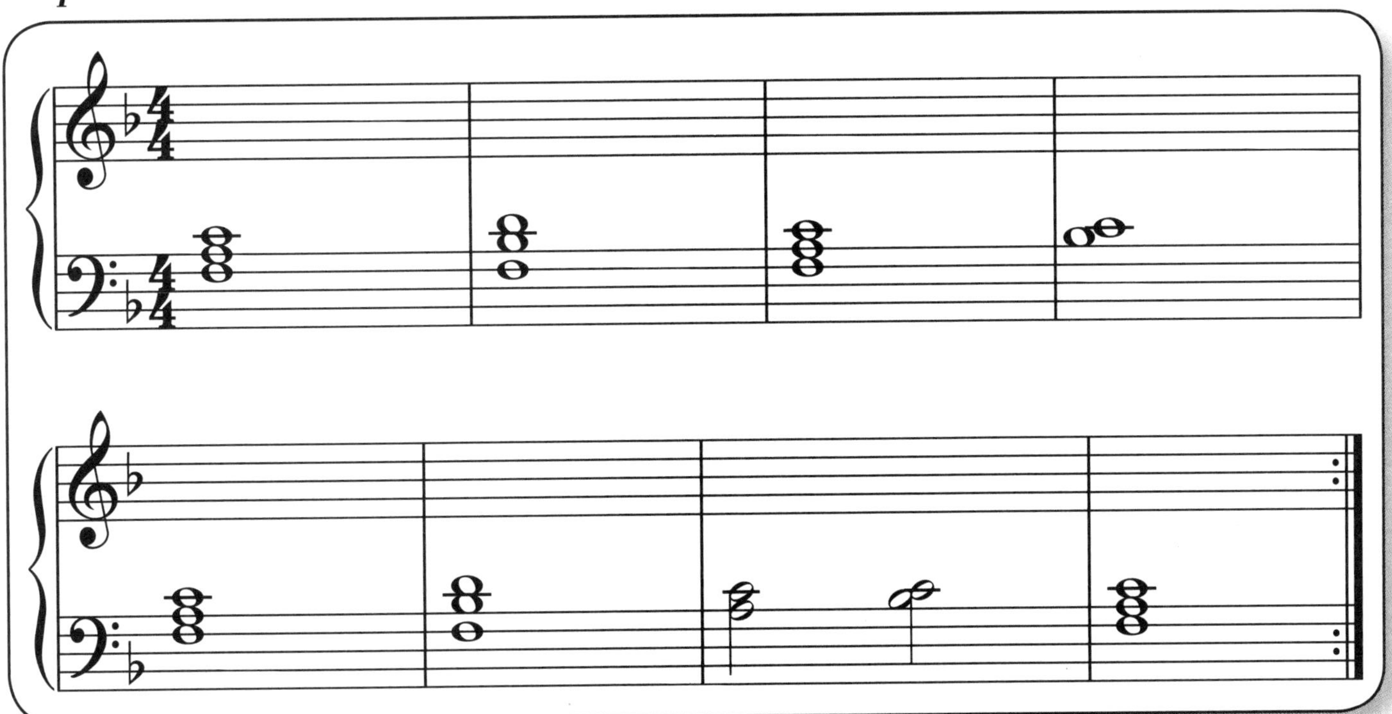

25a. Ready to Review

Primary chords are considered the strongest chords of a key. In major keys, these chords are always major and are built on the scale degrees 1, 4, and 5. Study the example below to learn the primary chords in the key of F major.

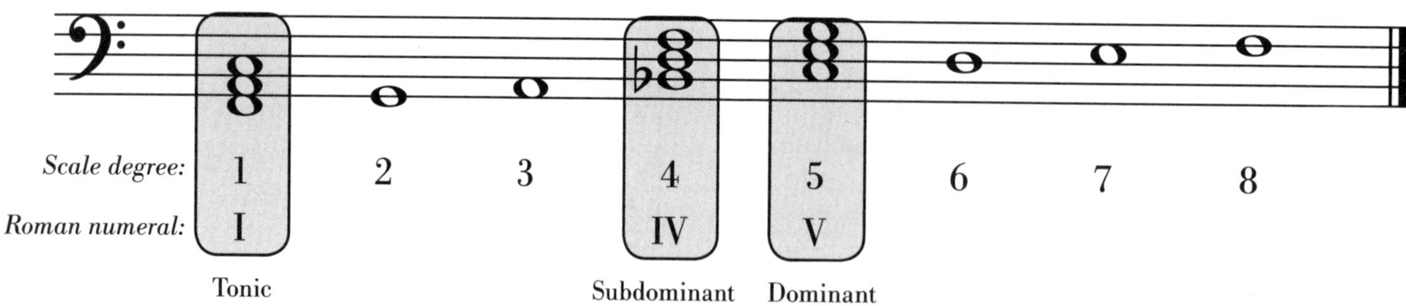

♫ ***Build primary chords (I, IV, V) in the keys of F major and G major.***

♫ The chord built on scale degree 1 is called the: **dominant** *or* **tonic**

♫ The chord built on scale degree 4 is called the: **tonic** *or* **subdominant**

♫ The chord built on scale degree 5 is called the: **dominant** *or* **tonic**

25b. Chord Progressions: F Major

♫ ***Practice the primary chord progressions in the key of F major.****

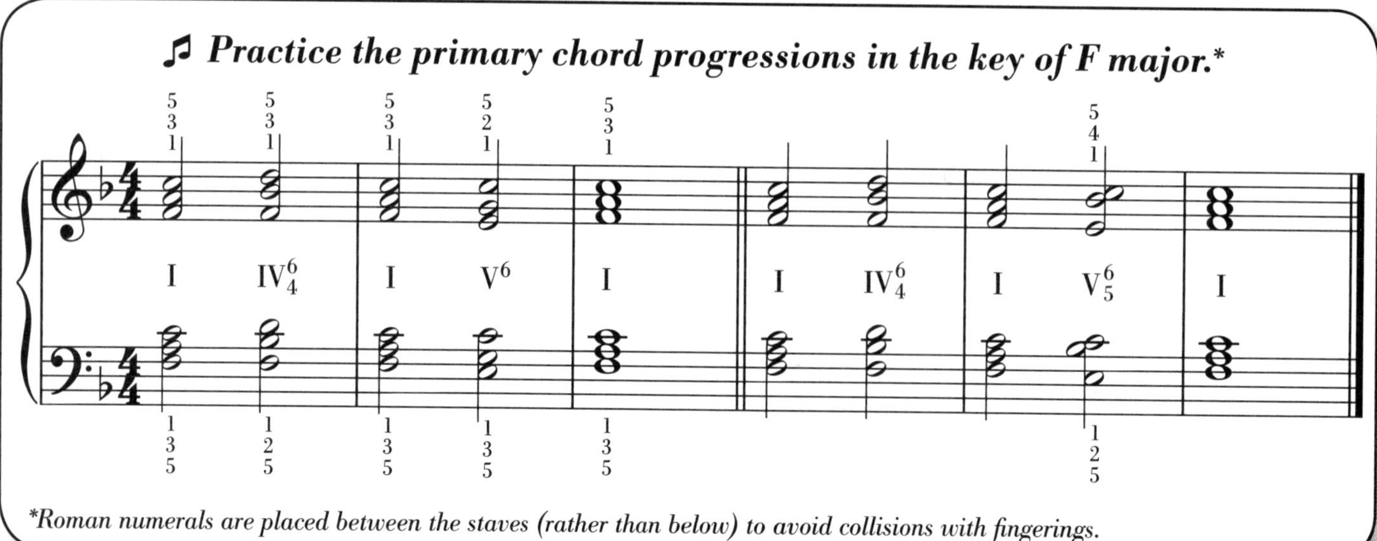

Roman numerals are placed between the staves (rather than below) to avoid collisions with fingerings.

25c. Power Play

♫ ***Add fingerings and then play the examples below.***

EXAMPLE 1:

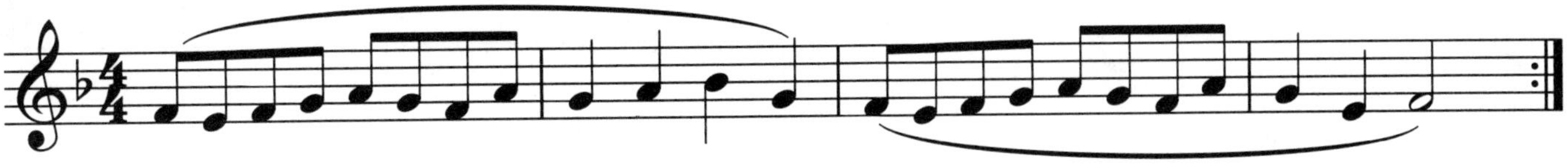

EXAMPLE 2:

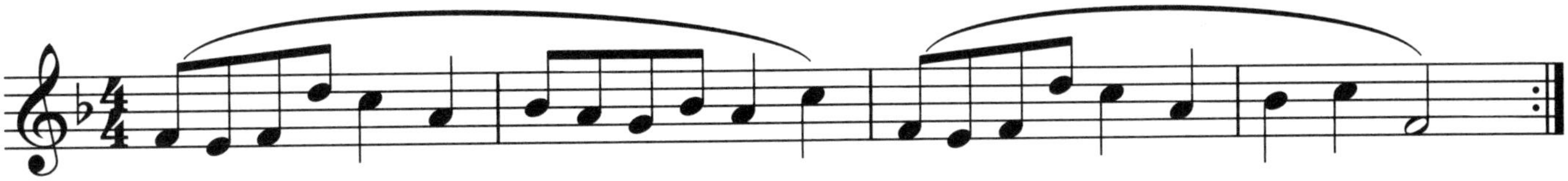

EXAMPLE 3:

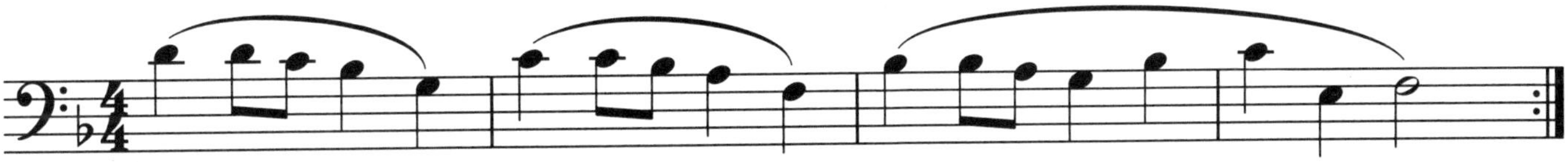

25d. I'm All Ears!

♫ ***Your teacher will play a major or minor triad. Notate the triad on the blank staff and label it above the staff with a chord symbol.****

1.

2.

3.

4.

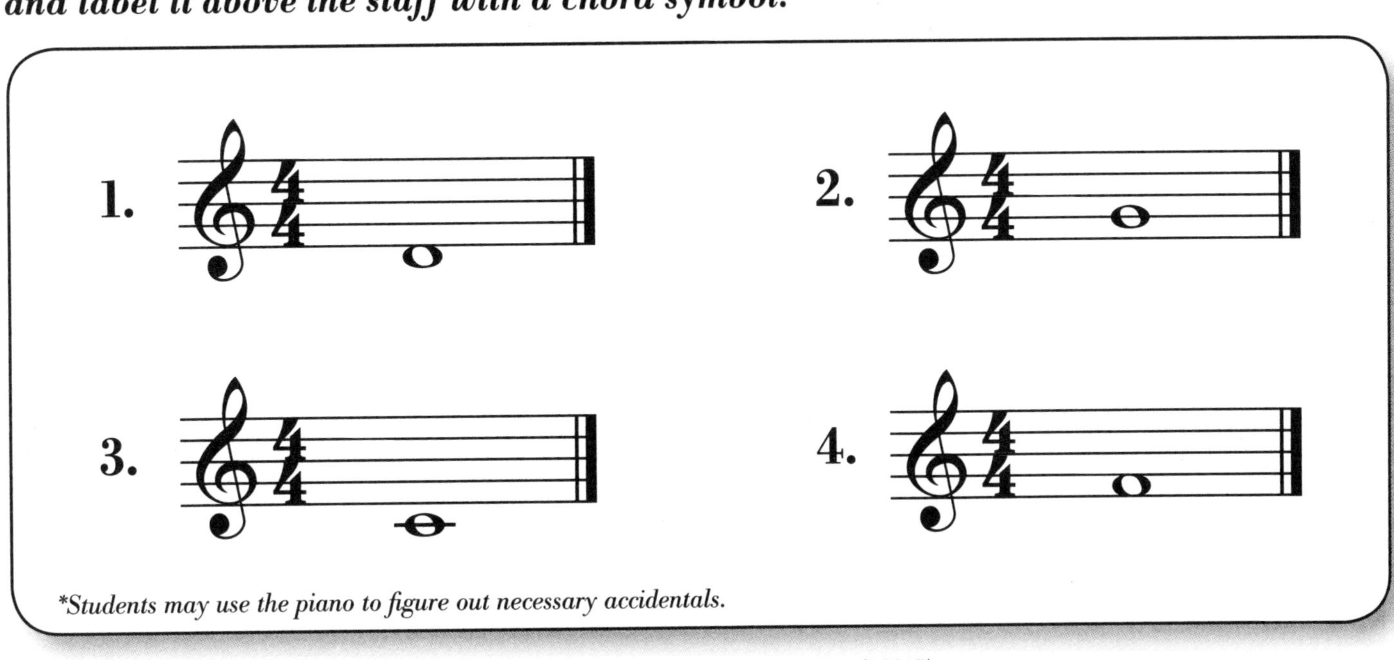

**Students may use the piano to figure out necessary accidentals.*

26a. Ready to Review

♫ *Label each interval as a major second (M2) or a minor second (m2).*

____ ____ ____ ____ ____ ____

♫ *Label each interval as a major third (M3) or a minor third (m3).*

____ ____ ____ ____ ____ ____

♫ *Label each interval as a perfect fourth (P4) or a perfect fifth (P5).*

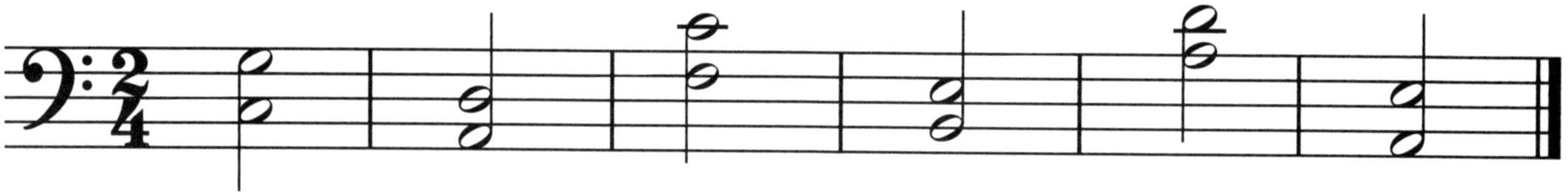

____ ____ ____ ____ ____ ____

♫ *Notate the chords indicated. Watch the clefs!*

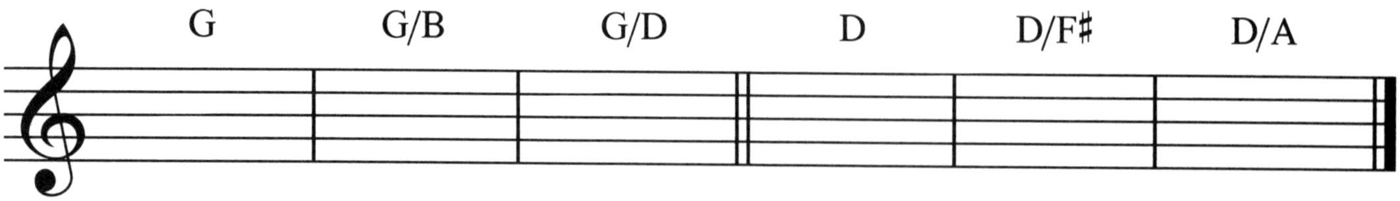

G G/B G/D D D/F♯ D/A

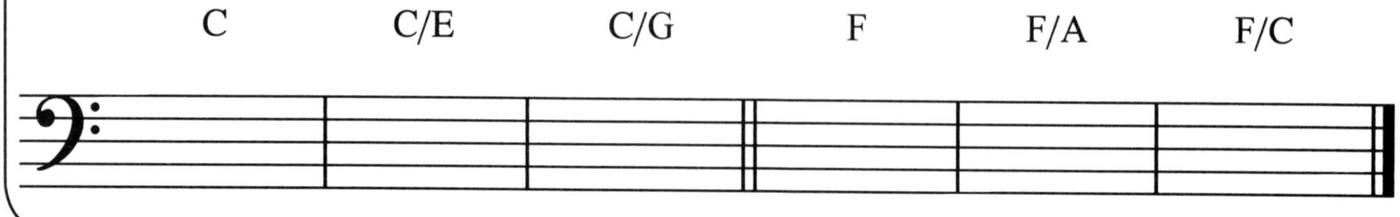

C C/E C/G F F/A F/C

26b. Power Play

♫ ***Play the examples below. Use the fingerings provided.***

EXAMPLE 1:

mp

EXAMPLE 2:

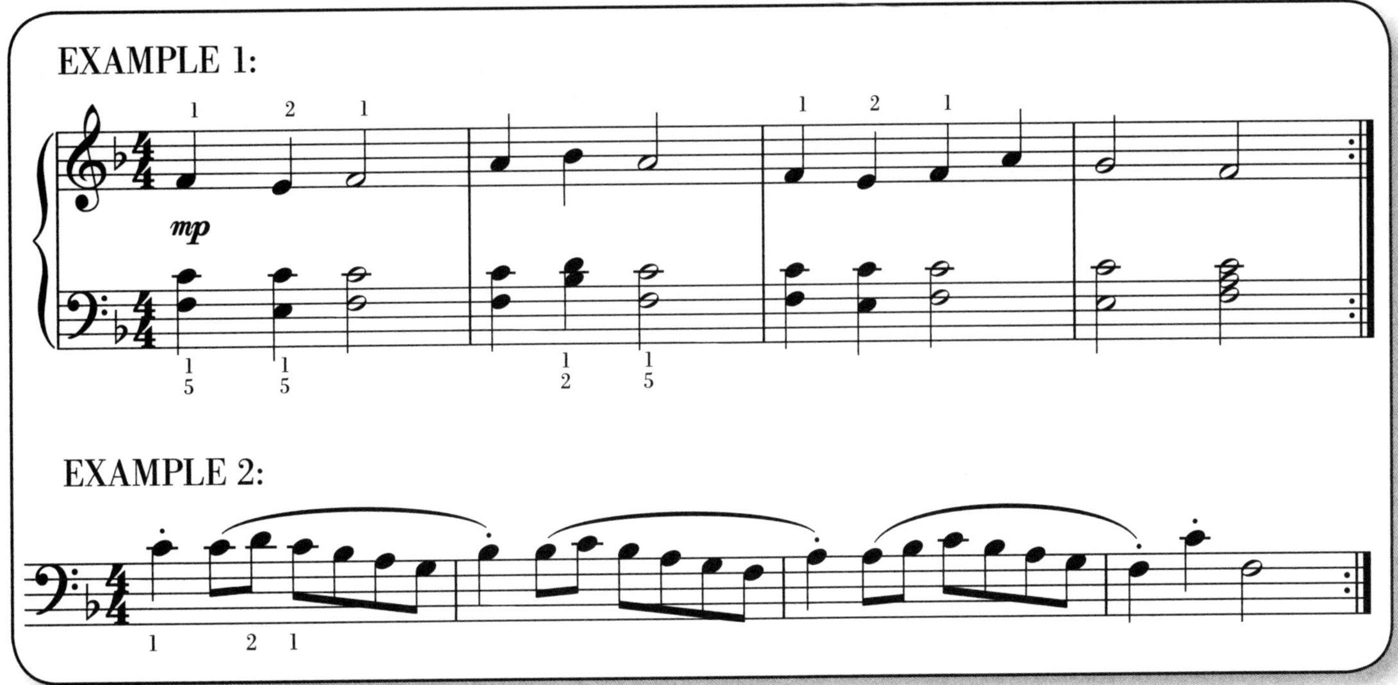

26c. Composition Corner

♫ ***Transpose the given melody to the key of C major on the staff below. Add the missing chord symbols, transposed to the new key, above the staff.***

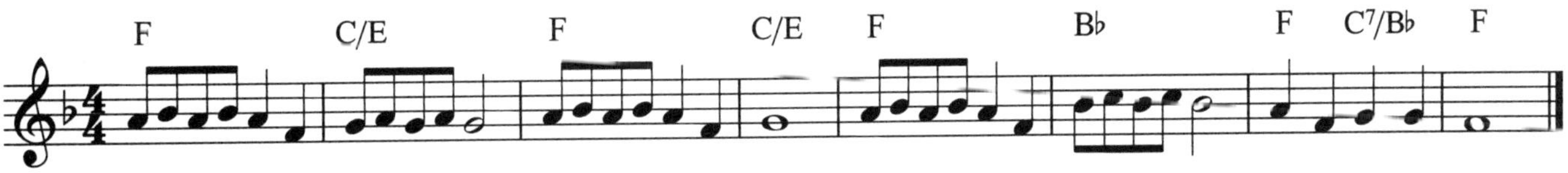
F
C/E
F
C/E
F
B♭
F
C7/B♭
F

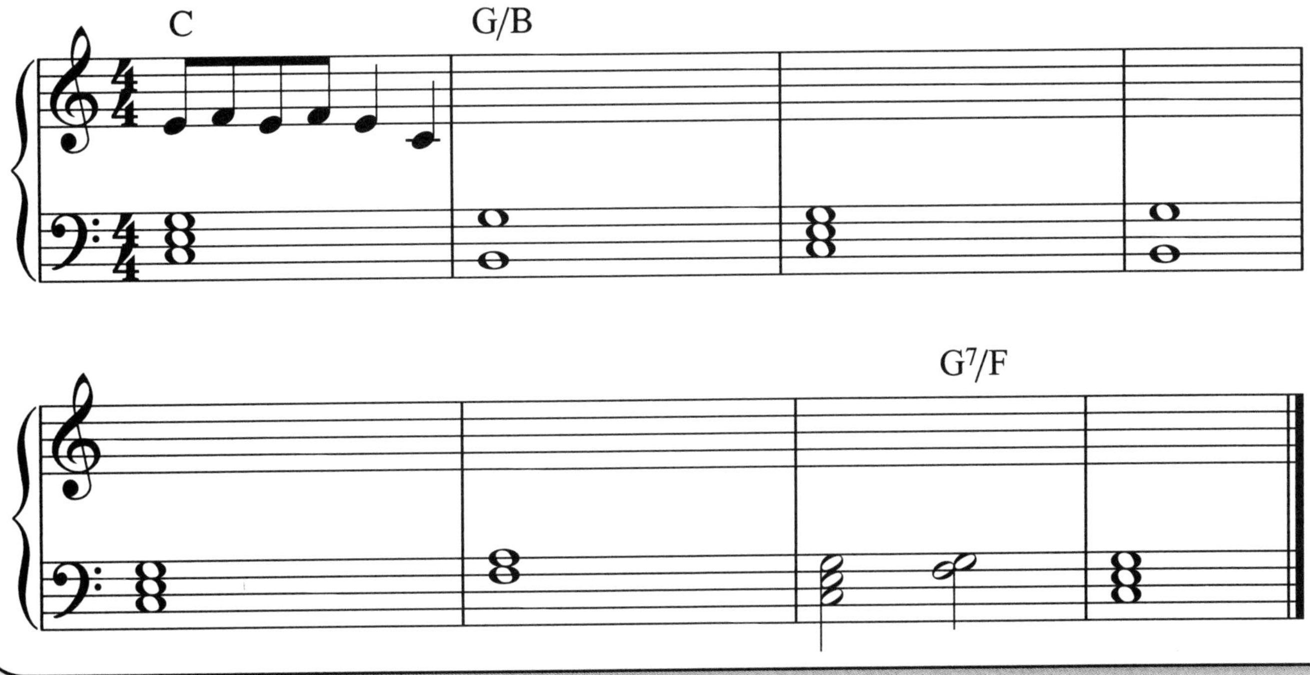
C
G/B
G7/F

27a. Ready to Review

♫ The pattern of whole steps and half steps used to build a major scale is:

______ ______ ______ ______ ______ ______ ______

♫ ***Notate the C major scale, in whole notes, on the staff below.***

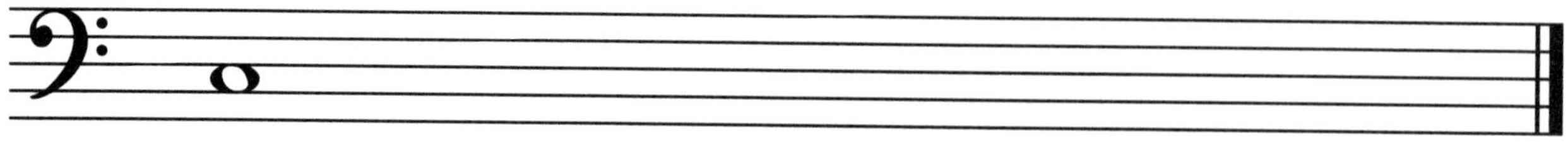

♫ ***Notate the G major scale, in whole notes, on the staff below.***

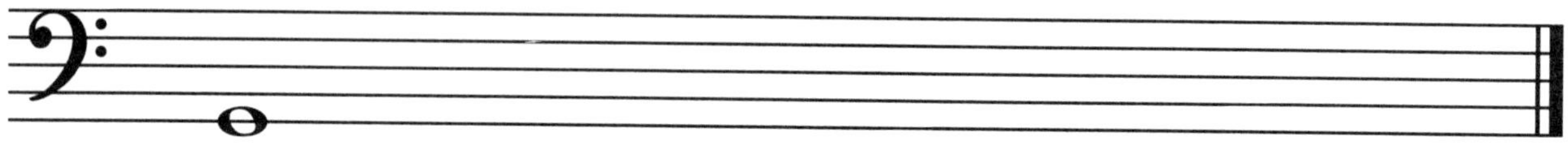

♫ ***Notate the F major scale, in whole notes, on the staff below.***

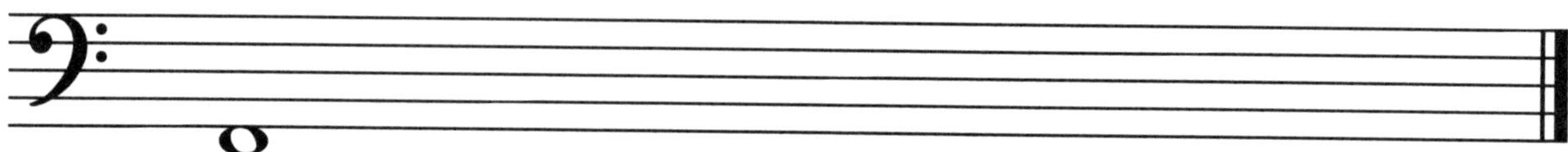

♫ ***Draw the key signatures.***

Key of F major

Key of C major

Key of G major

27b. Power Play

♫ Play the examples below. Use the fingerings provided.

EXAMPLE 1:

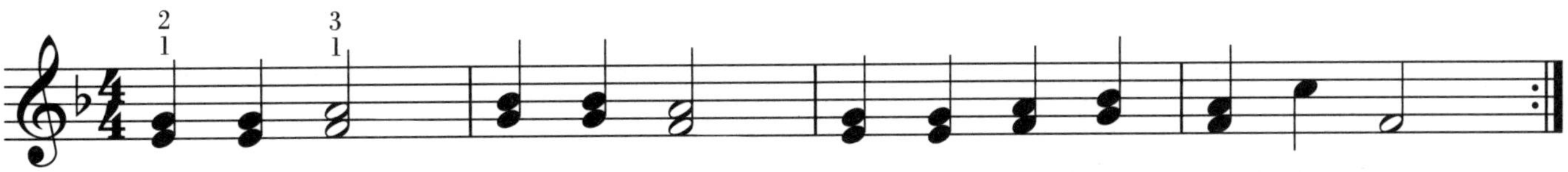

EXAMPLE 2:

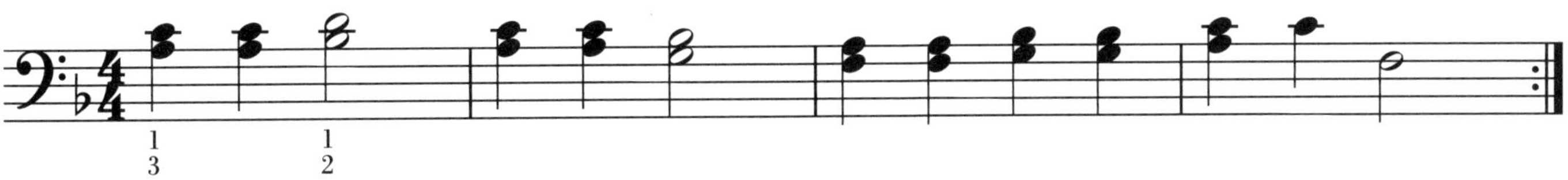

EXAMPLE 3:

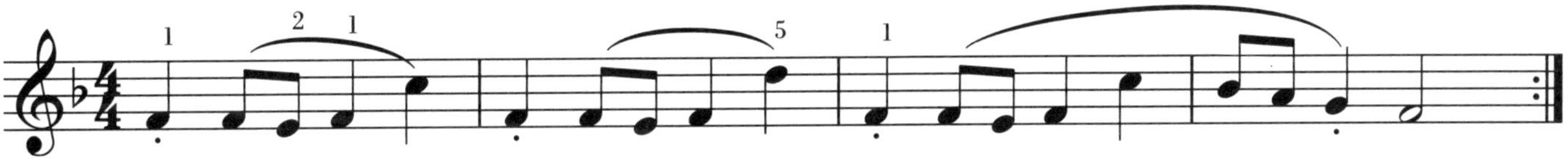

27c. I'm All Ears!

♫ Your teacher will play a major or minor triad. Notate the triad on the staff and label it above the staff with a chord symbol.

1.

2.

3.

4.

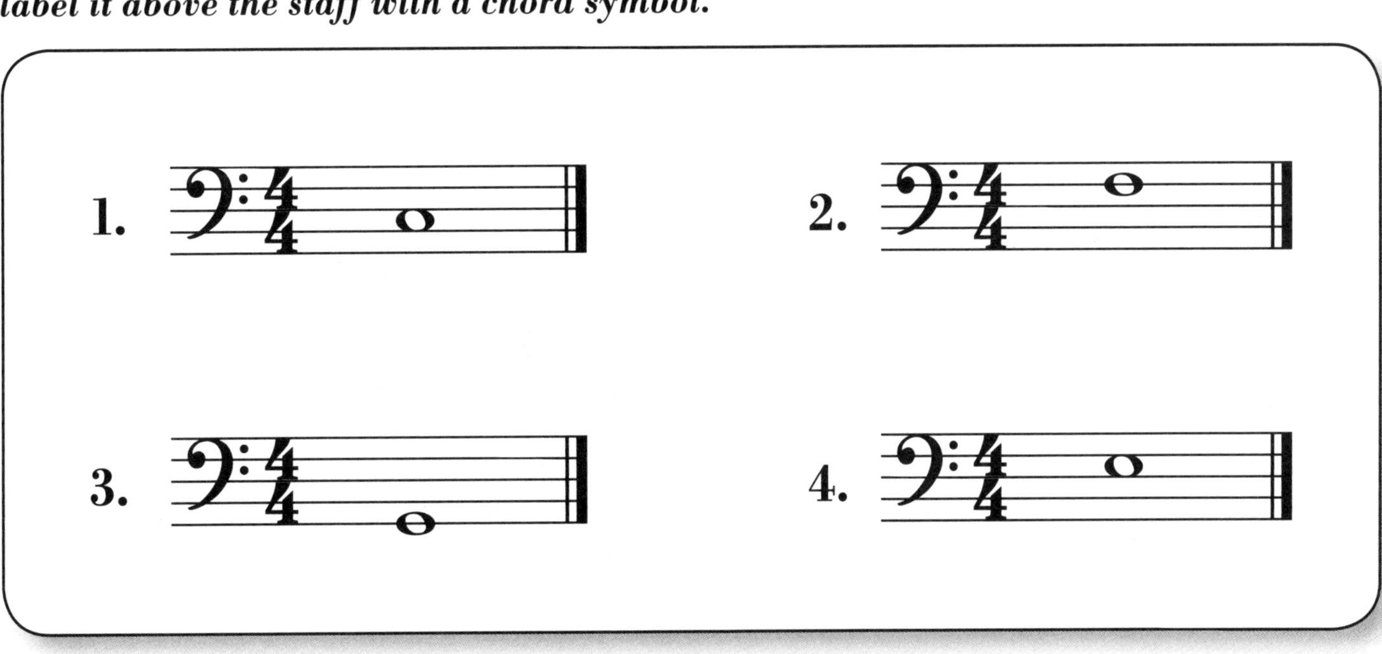

28a. Ready to Review

♫ *Draw the correct note or rest on the blank staff and fill in the beat numbers.**

Eighth note = ___ beat

Half rest = ___ beats of silence

Whole note = ___ beats

Quarter rest = ___ beat of silence

Dotted half note = ___ beats

Whole rest = ___ beats of silence

Eighth rest = ___ beat of silence

♫ *Match each tempo with the correct definition.*

Moderato	Very slowly
Andante	Moderately
Largo	Fast, lively
Allegro	Walking speed

**Assume a 4/4 time signature.*

28b. Power Play

♫ ***Play the examples below. Add pedal, changing the pedal every two beats.***

28c. Ahead of Schedule

Congratulations for reaching the end of the book! Let's celebrate by playing a final piece. It is written in a minor key and has a special "surprise" at the end.

Major Scales: Parallel Motion*

Key of C major:

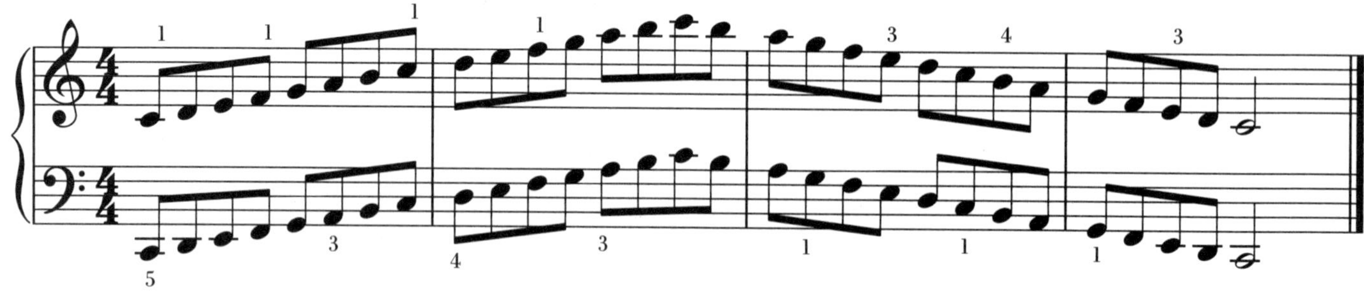

Key of G major:

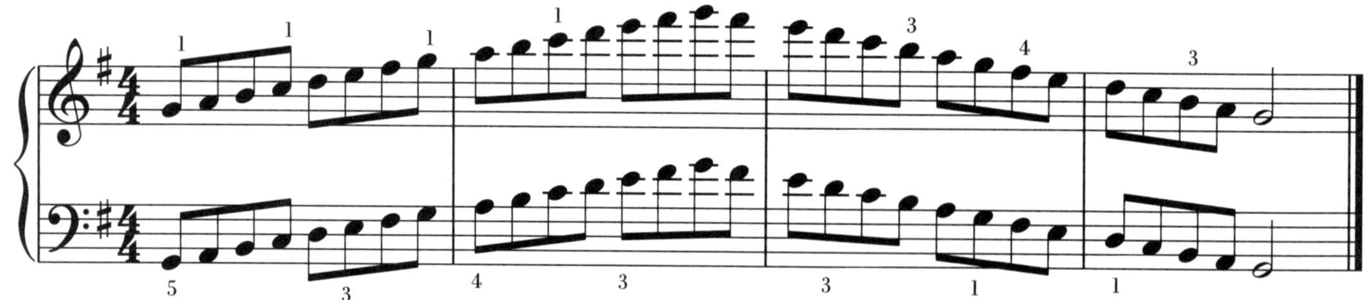

Key of F major:

**Octave adjustments can be made according to preference.*

Key of F major:

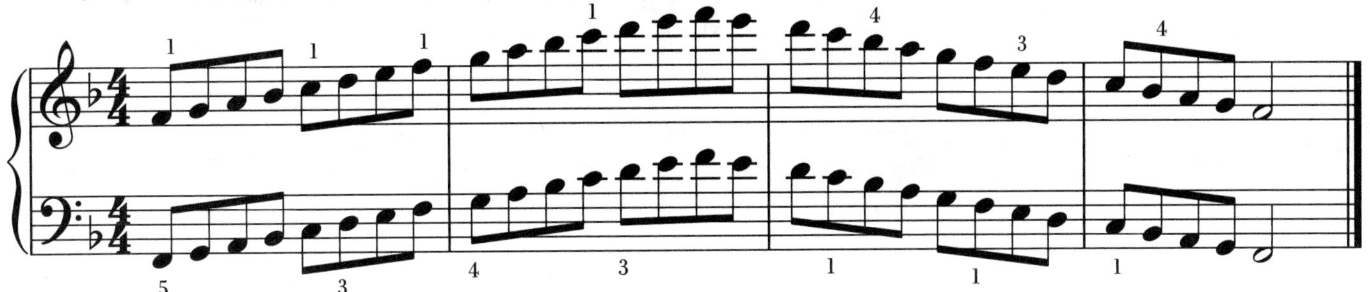

Primary Chord Progressions

Key of C major:

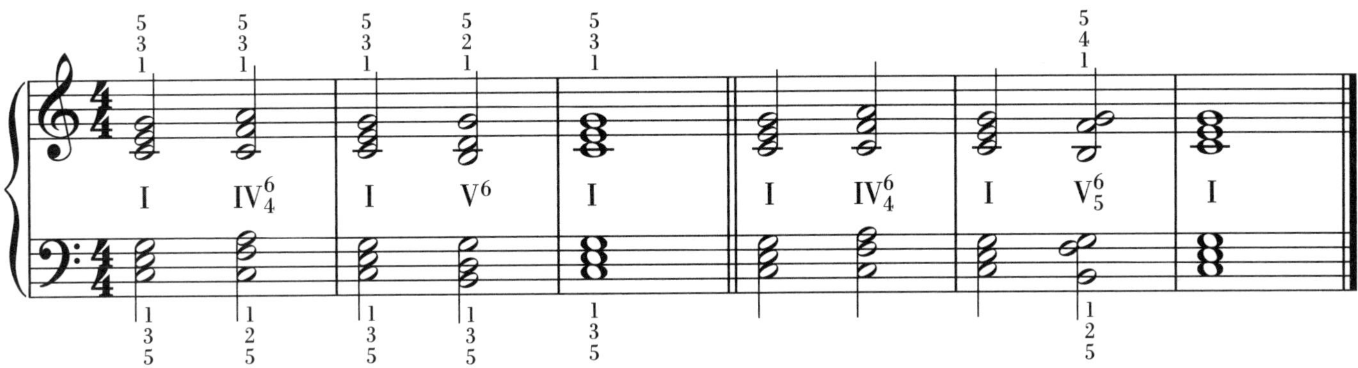

Key of G major:

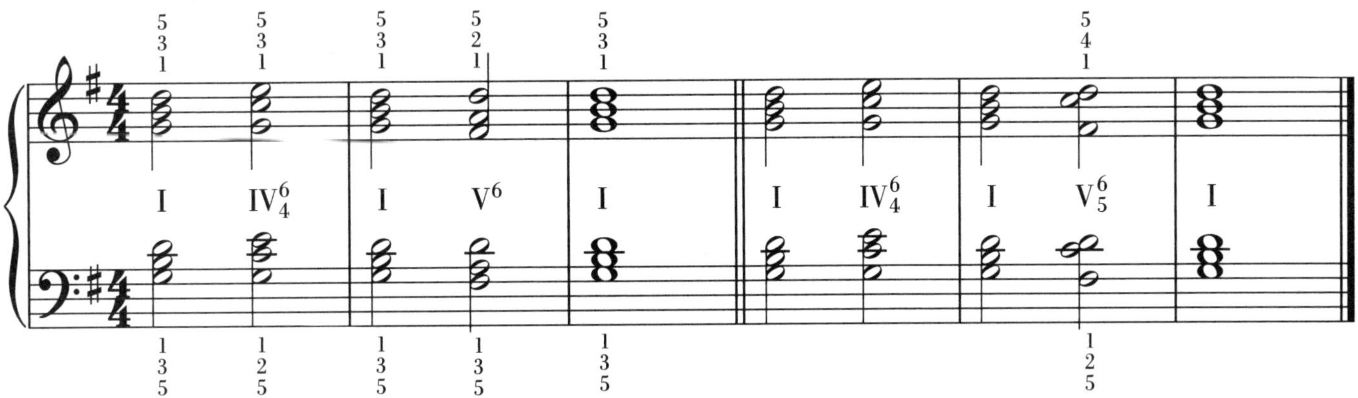

Key of F major:

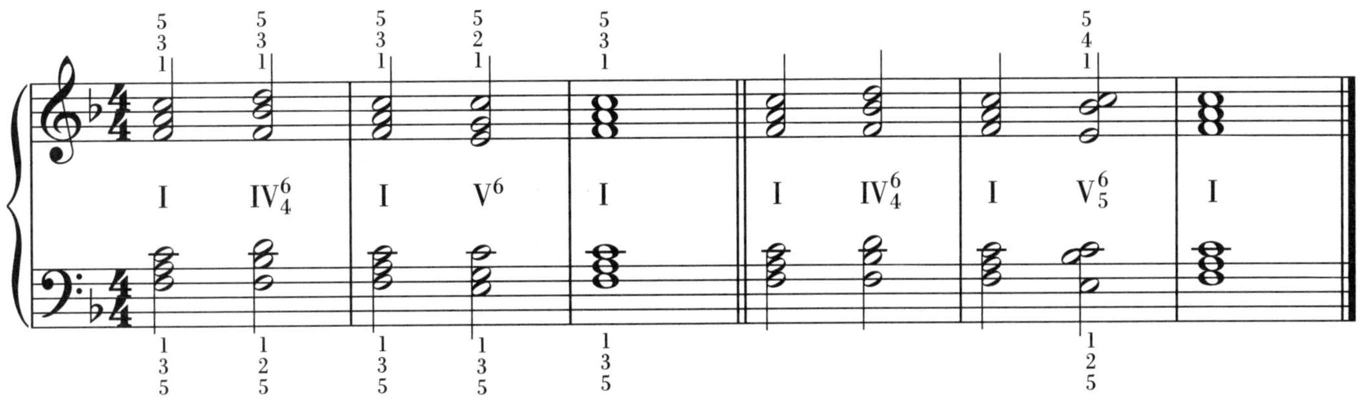

PIANO PRONTO
Certificate of Achievement
Congratulations to
(Student name)
for successfully completing Movement 1: Power Pages.
Jennifer Eklund
(Author of Piano Pronto)
Date of completion:
Teacher signature: